What Your Colleagues Are Saying . . .

ReLeah Lent has developed a great framework for helping content-area teachers think about their discipline-specific literacies. More important, she has equipped them with tools that allow them to *use* these literacies to forward content learning. From student-led discussions to reading infographics, *This Is Disciplinary Literacy* brings today's literacies into content classrooms.

—NANCY FREY
Co-Author of *Rigorous Reading* and
Text-Dependent Questions, Grades K–5 and *6–12*

This book makes me particularly hopeful. It is grounded in sound research and theory, but is wholly practical and accessible. It lays out a clear mandate (too long lost) to have students communicate as much as possible like experts in a discipline. It encourages teachers to join students in probing the capacity of each discipline, in its own way, to help students think, inquire, solve problems, collaborate—and answer the question "What is life, and who am I in it?" *This Is Disciplinary Literacy* encourages us as teachers to rediscover the complexities of teaching and learning and to reinvent our classrooms, ourselves, and our students.

—CAROL ANN TOMLINSON
Professor at Curry School of Education,
University of Virginia

Content-area teachers will be delighted to find their concerns regarding disciplinary literacy finally addressed with discipline-specific ways of integrating literacy that will help all students deepen their content learning. Teachers who've struggled with how to integrate literacy into their discipline or who are looking for fresh ideas for increasing literacy in their content area will find classroom-ready examples they will be able to use. What I like most about this book is the focus on literacy as a vehicle to enhance learning for *all* content areas.

Nationa

Acquiring skill in disciplinary literacy is essential for students to become college and career ready. *This Is Disciplinary Literacy* is a contribution to teachers everywhere striving to meet the needs of their students. This book hits the right balance between rationale for disciplinary literacy and providing useful approaches to use in each content-area instruction. The book will help teachers provide opportunities for deeper learning of content as well as a demonstration of rigorous reading, writing, thinking, and doing. Congratulations on a job well done by ReLeah Lent.

—**JUDITH IRVIN**
Executive Director of
the National Literacy Project

This Is Disciplinary Literacy is your go-to book for everything you need to know about this important topic. Lent expertly guides middle and high school teachers through an explanation of disciplinary literacy as well as how and why teaching and learning approaches differ in each content area. Overflowing with examples from diverse classrooms and practical suggestions that teachers will embrace, chapters dedicated to reading, writing, inquiry, and collaborative learning will deepen your understanding of what literacy means in *your* subject.

—**LAURA ROBB**
Author of *Vocabulary Is Comprehension*

THIS IS

Disciplinary Literacy

READING, WRITING, THINKING, AND DOING... CONTENT AREA BY CONTENT AREA

RELEAH COSSETT LENT

FOREWORD BY CAROL ANN TOMLINSON

http://resources.corwin.com/lentDL

CL CORWIN
LITERACY

FOR INFORMATION:

Corwin

A SAGE Company

2455 Teller Road

Thousand Oaks, California 91320

(800) 233-9936

www.corwin.com

SAGE Publications Ltd.

1 Oliver's Yard

55 City Road

London EC1Y 1SP

United Kingdom

SAGE Publications India Pvt. Ltd.

B 1/I 1 Mohan Cooperative Industrial Area

Mathura Road, New Delhi 110 044

India

SAGE Publications Asia-Pacific Pte. Ltd.

3 Church Street

#10-04 Samsung Hub

Singapore 049483

Publisher: Lisa Luedeke

Editorial Development Manager: Julie Nemer

Assistant Editor: Emeli Warren

Production Editor: Melanie Birdsall

Copy Editor: Diane DiMura

Typesetter: C&M Digitals (P) Ltd.

Proofreader: Caryne Brown

Indexer: Maria Sosnowski

Cover and Interior Designer: Rose Storey

Marketing Managers: Maura Sullivan and
Rebecca Eaton

Printed in the United States of America

ISBN 978-1-5063-0669-8

This book is printed on acid-free paper.

SFI label applies to text stock

17 18 19 10 9 8 7 6

CONTENTS

Visit the companion website at
http://resources.corwin.com/lentDL
for downloadable resources, including a
Professional Learning Guide and PowerPoint® slides.

ACKNOWLEDGMENTS

My thanks go to the many teachers and students who contributed to this book by sharing their ideas, suggestions, and photographs. It has been a true collaborative effort, and I appreciate every single person who helped bring the text to life through such quality classroom examples. A special thanks goes to the talented teachers from the literacy cohorts at Barrington 220, where I have been engaged in a residency for several years. I especially appreciate the efforts of Nick Yeager, whose work with students continues to inspire me, and to my coaching partner there, Marsha Voigt, whose insights, recommendations, and contributions made this a much richer book.

Not often enough it seems, synchronistic events come together at exactly the right time to make an important difference. A snowstorm prevented me from keynoting the Kentucky Council of Teachers of English's conference on the first day of the event, and the organizers postponed my talk until the second day. As I describe in Chapter 6, while waiting to speak, I stumbled into a session that eventually became the missing piece for this book. Thank you Brent Peters, Joe Franzen, and all of the students from Fern Creek who talked with me, shared their passions, and motivated me to "show not tell" a real story about disciplinary literacy in action. A special thank-you goes to Quinten Stephenson for taking me on an outside tour of the school on a freezing morning in February and for answering my endless questions. As an aside, if you want to feel good about education in America, visit Fern Creek Traditional High School in Louisville, Kentucky.

And while it is customary to acknowledge the editorial, marketing, and production team that come together to create a book, my gratitude goes way beyond what is merely expected. The team at Corwin are caring and experienced professionals who work tirelessly to make it right. Thank you to my friend and editor Lisa Luedeke for her talented guidance in shaping this book from beginning to end, Maura Sullivan for providing the best marketing in the business, Julie Nemer and Rose Storey for my eye-popping cover, Melanie Birdsall for seeing the book through production, Diane DiMura for making the copyediting almost fun, and especially to Emeli Warren for her encouragement and incredible organizational skills as we fit the many pieces of the book together into a coherent whole.

Finally, thanks to my father, whose keen engineering mind identified some rather significant omissions and to my husband and mentor, Bert, who kept me sane once again during this whole crazy process.

Publisher's Acknowledgments

Corwin gratefully acknowledges the contributions of the following reviewers:

Lynn M. Angus
K–12 English Language Arts
    Curriculum Coordinator
DeKalb County School District
Decatur, GA

Jayne Ellspermann
High School Principal
2015 NASSP National
    Principal of the Year
West Port High School
Ocala, FL

Mike Rafferty
Curriculum Leader for LA/Reading PK–5
Fairfield Public Schools
Fairfield, CT

Terrell S. Tracy
Assistant Professor of Education and
    Director of EdS in Literacy
Converse College
Spartanburg, SC

Marsha Voigt
Educational Consultant
    and Literacy Coach
Affiliated with District 220
Barrington, IL

Jennifer Wheat-Townsend
Director of Learning
Noblesville Schools
Noblesville, IN

FOREWORD

The two decades I spent in public school classrooms were at a particularly fertile time in education—or at least so it seems to me. Shortly after I began teaching, cognitive psychology became the driver of educational conversations and planning, replacing behaviorism, which had been in the driver's seat for a good long time. For the first time, there was broad emphasis on students as meaning makers, inquirers, and problem solvers rather than parrot-like creatures who should be trained to repeat what they've heard. Cognition triumphed over regurgitation during those years.

My colleagues and I spent much time and energy discussing models of thinking and integrating them into our instructional plans. Paideia Seminars, problem-based learning, Webquests, product-focused instruction, models that support divergent thinking, and interdisciplinary instruction were increasingly common classroom approaches as we sought to help our students grow in autonomy as thinkers. Students were generally the primary "doers" in classrooms, energized by tasks that often seemed linked to the world beyond school. Teachers were energized by students' enthusiasm and by learning how to be catalysts for student thinking.

During the last few years of my secondary school teaching career, I went to graduate school while I continued teaching. I did not go because I wanted a different job.

I adored teaching in the middle school where I'd been for much of my career. Rather, I went because there were so many things that seemed important to learn about how to create dynamic, student-centered classrooms. I knew a degree program would give me the opportunity to learn and deadlines that would encourage me to read and think at a level difficult for a teacher to accomplish without an imposed discipline.

During that time, I read a book by Philip H. Phenix called *Realms of Meaning*, and it was revolutionary in my growth as a teacher. It was certainly not an easy read, but its message provided a way of thinking about curriculum that was new to me and that turned my world upside down. Phenix reflected that for much of early human history, people had no time for much beyond survival—hunting, building fires for cooking and keeping predators at bay, seeking shelter. As we progressed, however, and began to have a bit of leisure time, Phenix explained, humans became more reflective. We began to ask a question that people ever since have been born asking, and have died asking. The question is, "What is life, and who am I in it?" The disciplines, says Phenix, were created to answer that question. History exists to answer the question "What is life, and who am I in it?" Science likewise exists to answer that question, as does math, literature, the arts, and so on. Each discipline is designed to answer that same question, but through its own unique lens.

A light switch flipped on in my mind, and I was seized by two polar realizations. I was teaching English (or literature, or language arts) as a collection of information. I taught novels and stories and dramas as exercises in recognizing plot, setting, character, theme, protagonist, antagonist, figures of speech, and so on. No author ever struggled to birth words and ideas so English teachers could reduce their work to that level. I needed to teach literature as an answer to the question "What is life, and who am I in it?"! I taught writing as a relatively prescribed, stepwise progress—not as an opportunity to understand our lives and our place in a wider world. I had to do better by my students—and the generations of writers who understood writing as an exploration of life and its significance. I began to understand the reality that, while important, content is not enough, and that, while imperative, process in isolation from content is crippled. It began to be clear to me that students must use knowledge and processes as disciplinarians would use them—to develop products that answer nagging questions, share insights, and create new knowledge.

I began to understand slowly what it meant to teach "according to the nature of the discipline." My classes changed dramatically. My students changed dramatically. I changed dramatically. And all of those were profound improvements.

Right about that time, the first state-mandated standards and high-stakes tests appeared on the horizon. I felt at the time, and still feel, that schools very shortly thereafter entered a sort of educational Dark Age. It was as though cognitive psychology (and emergent neuroscience) had been banished and replaced with a fundamental form of behaviorism. In a stunningly brief time, students were once again cast as parrots, teachers were rewarded for training the parrots well, and curriculum was a collection of data to be committed to memory and repeated on demand.

In *The Act of Creation*, Arthur Koestler suggests that we sometimes replace an anthropomorphic view of a rat with a "rattomorphic" view of man. One of my university students recently wrote that American schools have been functioning with a "rattomorphic" view of a learner as a being that can be taught mechanically and interchangeably. I appreciated his analogy. It spoke to a feeling I have struggled with for the last fifteen years, give or take, when teaching has felt much like training a rat to get through a maze and learning has resembled running the maze. We lost the disciplines as they are meant to be. We lost thinking, inquiring, cognition and metacognition, student agency and independence. We abandoned the nature of the disciplines. We lost the essence of what it means to be human—and *understanding* what it means to be human.

Sometimes now, I hear echoes of those things stirring back to life in classrooms and books and blogs and videos and teacher conversations—and I am hopeful. *This* book makes me particularly hopeful. It is grounded in sound research and theory, but is wholly practical and accessible. It lays out a clear mandate (too long lost) to have students communicate as much as possible like experts in a discipline. It helps us develop a clearer sense of how communication varies across disciplines in order to meet the distinct demands of the different disciplines. It encourages teachers to join students in probing the capacity of each discipline, in its own way, to help students think, inquire, solve problems, collaborate—and answer the question "What is life, and who am I in it?" The book provides clear and actionable guidelines and tools. More to the point, it encourages us as teachers to rediscover the complexities of teaching and learning—*really* teaching and *really* learning—and in that way, to reinvent our classrooms, ourselves, and our profession.

That's something worth feeling excited about. It's been too long, but it's not too late.

—**Carol Ann Tomlinson, EdD**
William Clay Parrish, Jr., Professor and Chair
Educational Leadership, Foundations, and Policy
Curry School of Education
University of Virginia

LITERACY *WITHIN* THE DISCIPLINES

Reading *across* the content areas? Every teacher a teacher of writing? Not so fast. Current thinking about literacy places reading and writing in its rightful place, firmly rooted *within* each discipline. This new model, aptly called "Disciplinary Literacy," recognizes that reading, writing, thinking, reasoning, and *doing* within each discipline is unique—and leads to the understanding that every field of study creates, communicates, and evaluates knowledge differently. As such, each content-area teacher is responsible for showing students how to use discipline-specific literacy skills as tools for accessing content and, with a sigh of relief, incorporating reading strategies only when they make sense within the context of the discipline.

How does this approach different from the old "content-area reading" approach? As an example, let's look at a skill needed for comprehension of most texts, making an inference. Using the content-area reading approach, every teacher might use the same strategy to teach students how to make an inference—a two-column chart, perhaps, with "What the Author Says" in one column and "What the Author Means" in the opposing column. But we're learning that it's not quite that simple. Understanding inferences in history might require that the reader infer the perspectives of primary and secondary documents regarding the same event. Such a process requires a different approach than when making an inference in English language arts (ELA) where students must "read between the lines" to interpret the actions of a character or untangle a metaphor. And an inference in science might look more like a hypothesis with data to back up the hunch. An inference is far less nuanced in math, relying more on discernible patterns than on interpretation.

Along with this more reasonable approach comes a sense of empowerment for content-area teachers. Those who never felt qualified to teach "reading"—and said so from the beginning—can now feel confident in their abilities to teach literacy as it relates to their discipline.

As I put the finishing touches on this book, Nancie Atwell, the legendary teacher and author who put reading and writing workshops on the map, has just won the Varkey Foundation's first Global Teacher Prize with an award of one million dollars. During an interview on CNN, she discussed *disciplinary literacy,* though she didn't use that phrase. She talked about how her students are given time in class each day to practice reading and writing—the "doing" of her discipline. She said of her students, "They are authentic readers and writers. They read and write the way you [the interviewers] do. Because they do, they know what reading and writing are good for." Imagine if students in all disciplines were authentically "doing the work" and developing the academic habits of those in the field. Education would be transformed.

The Problem With Reading Strategies

For many years, reading strategies have dominated the literacy scene. Just open the pages of any teacher's edition, and you'll find whole

Those who never felt qualified to teach "reading"—and said so from the beginning—can now feel confident in their abilities to teach literacy as it relates to their discipline.

sections devoted to every strategy imaginable—and then some. While reading strategies can certainly help students unlock difficult text, the pendulum swung too far, as is often the case in education, and the strategy at times became more important than the content. Students were tested on how well they used strategies (ten sticky notes equals an A, for instance), and many schools even jumped on the strategy-of-the-week bandwagon.

Strategies can be shortcuts through content because they are generic to *any* text, primarily used for the purpose of creating better readers and writers overall who, incidentally, might then score higher on standardized tests. But as far as disciplinary learning goes, strategies don't always live up to their reputation. In fact, despite the wholesale strategy blitz, American high school seniors showed no improvement in their reading abilities in four years, according to the latest National Assessment of Educational Progress (NAEP).

What we are coming to understand is that readers must know something about the content in order to use a strategy effectively. Science teachers, especially, argue that students may apply the strategy to perfection but have no conceptual understanding of the content due to a topic's complexity.

Echoing this thought, National Council of Teachers of English's (NCTE) Policy Research Brief on Literacies of Disciplines (2011) quotes researcher Elizabeth Moje as saying, "Strategies—absent some level of knowledge, a purpose for engaging in the literate practice and an identification with the domain or the purpose—will not take readers or writers very far" (p. 2).

STRATEGY FATIGUE FOR TEACHERS

The difficulty with strategies turned out to be twofold. First, as noted earlier, general across-the-curriculum strategies frequently turned into exercises rather than thoughtful tools for reading. Students were not always taught when to use the strategy or how to adapt it to disciplinary text. Making a prediction about what a character will do next could help some ELA students better understand internal conflict, just as making a prediction in science could help students more actively engage with an experiment; but asking a student in social studies to make a prediction without background knowledge or context about where a certain country is located might well be a waste of instructional time. Rather than just plugging in preselected reading strategies, we want kids thinking about *what* and *how* they are reading. Second, teaching strategies in isolation often strains an already overburdened curriculum. This "one more thing to do" approach is understandably frustrating, often ineffective, and has at times created resentment among content teachers who may feel literacy is the job of the ELA or reading teacher.

Shifting the paradigm into a more discipline-based approach helps all teachers understand that literacy is an inherent part of each discipline, one that *supports* content learning. And who knows better how to show students the literacy skills fundamental to a specific discipline than the content-area teacher? Students then walk away with more than a bag full of strategies. They come to know how reading, writing, speaking, and thinking function in each discipline and are able to gather multiple perspectives about the role of literacy, creating a flexible "culture of literacy" that will serve them well in college or career.

Unpacking Disciplinary Literacy

The working definition of *literacy* has changed as much as this new approach to it. Turning again to NCTE's Policy Research Brief on Literacies of Disciplines (2011), we read that "literacy is not a single or monolithic entity. Rather it is a set of multi-faceted social practices that are shaped by contexts, participants, and technologies" (p. 1). Literacy was once thought to be a set of skills necessary for reading and writing, but we have now moved far beyond the printed page to include in our definition of texts anything that helps us make meaning, whether in visual, audio, or multimodal format. And those social practices mentioned in NCTE's document begin in the classroom, extend to the family and the workplace, and continue throughout the entire global community. That's why there is a renewed interest in collaborative learning, which I address in Chapter 5.

To complicate a description of literacy that is just starting to make sense, both literacy and texts look different in various disciplines. The most

Teachers must move from transmitting information to showing students how to engage in the literacies that make up their discipline.

obvious example in the four major disciplines is literacy in math, which cannot truly be compared to literacy in any other content area. Other subjects such as the arts rely on extremely specialized texts: "musical scores, lighting diagrams, human bodies, conductors, and other signs [are] used to represent meaning" says Roni Jo Draper (2015) in an article on disciplinary literacy. "As such, the definition of literacy . . . consists of the ability to use texts in discipline-appropriate ways or in ways that disciplinary experts would recognize as correct" (p. 59).

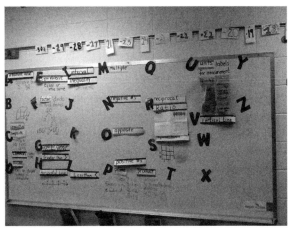

Tina Reckamp

Tina Reckamp's students create a word wall that utilizes the language of math.

The University of Pittsburgh's Learning Research and Development Center has been working with disciplinary literacy since 2002 and has even developed a model for its use in the content areas. Their definition of the term is comprehensive and best represents what I mean when I discuss disciplinary literacy: "Disciplinary Literacy involves the use of reading, reasoning, investigating, speaking, and writing required to learn and form complex content knowledge appropriate to a particular discipline" (McConachie, 2010, p. 16).

Moje (2008) layers another dimension to the definition when she argues that disciplinary learning doesn't just build knowledge but actually produces or constructs it.

Based on these understandings, it's clear that we have a lot of work to do within the disciplines because constructing knowledge requires skills that go much deeper than teaching students to employ reading strategies or fill in a bubble on a test. It means that teachers must move from transmitting information to showing students how to engage in the literacies that make up their discipline. This approach involves a different vision of what it means to teach, one that doesn't just show students how to read but how to critique what they are reading, doesn't just expect students to find evidence but what to do with that evidence, and doesn't just parcel out knowledge but asks students to use knowledge in meaningful and relevant ways.

Deeper Learning and Disciplinary Literacy

Disciplinary literacy is not the application of strategies to the disciplines; it is a way of learning that drills deeply into the very essence of what it means to come to know content.

One of the reasons that disciplinary literacy is so important is that it has everything to do with deeper learning, a phrase many researchers and educators use to encompass more familiar terms such as *critical thinking, higher order thinking,* and the now ubiquitous *rigor.* The first column in Figure 1.1 shows the attributes of deeper learning from The Hewlett Foundation (n.d.); the second column reflects their relationship to disciplinary literacy. The application in italics explains how deeper learning might look in a disciplinary literacy (DL) classroom.

We see once again that disciplinary literacy is not the application of strategies to the disciplines; it is a way of learning that drills deeply into the very essence of what it means to come to know content.

Disciplinary Literacy and Standards

For administrators and teachers who are working with the Common Core State Standards (CCSS; also Common Core) as a way to ground literacy within the disciplines, this approach makes perfect sense. Best of all, it honors the expertise of content-area teachers who may be resistant to the standards' literacy "push." Instead of treating each standard as an isolated learning target to be posted and checked off, this model weaves literacy into the basic fabric of content, satisfying the intent of the standards and the goals of teachers.

In any case, there is plenty of evidence to support the use of disciplinary literacy within the Common Core as well as within 21st century learning initiatives and the standards several states have adopted in place of Common Core. Not only is literacy emphasized in every state's standards,

Figure 1.1

The Connection Between Deeper Learning and Disciplinary Literacy

Deeper Learning	Disciplinary Literacy
Results in the mastery of core academic content	Results in the mastery of core academic content by developing expertise in specific disciplines
Application: Students master content by engaging in the habits of thinking and "work" of the discipline.	
Employs critical thinking and problem solving	Employs critical thinking and problem solving by engaging in the methods and inquiries of a discipline
Application: Students employ creative and critical thinking to identify and solve discipline-specific problems.	
Relies on collaboration	Relies on collaboration within the classroom community that mirrors the work done by those in the field
Application: Students learn how to become self-directed within a team as they plan, share, and assess learning within a discipline.	
Fosters an academic mindset	Fosters an academic discipline-specific mindset by learning and experiencing the foundational facts, skills, norms, and habits within a discipline
Application: Students find meaning as it relates to the discipline as they wrestle with project plans, disciplinary principles, and demonstrations of learning.	
Is supported through communication in writing and speaking	Is supported through communication in writing and speaking as discipline-specific tools for engaging in the work of the discipline
Application: Students learn how to use writing and speaking as they act as apprentices in a given discipline.	

but disciplinary learning is addressed in corresponding standards, such as The Next Generation Science Standards. If you aren't convinced, read Michael Manderino and Corrine Wickens' 2014 article from the *Illinois Reading Council Journal* titled "Addressing Disciplinary Literacy in the Common Core Standards" and use their analysis as justification for redefining literacy in content-area study.

It's also worth noting here that researchers have been writing about disciplinary literacy for some time but, as always, it takes a while for practice to catch up with research. In education, it may be even more difficult to make such a transition, not only because of the vastness of a system populated with students unique to every classroom in every state but, let's face it, also because of the long fingers of politicians who sometimes make decisions not in the best interest of teachers or students. As this new paradigm takes hold, however, I predict a shift by policymakers to view literacy as a natural outgrowth of disciplinary learning.

The Role of the Teacher

But where do content-area teachers begin? How do they step back from "presenting" content and begin to infuse literacy skills into every class, every day, so that students can produce and not just memorize information? It's true that professional development must target disciplinary "ways of knowing" instead of generic reading strategies, but teachers also must be given permission to use their professional expertise, preferably within professional learning communities (PLCs) or with colleagues, in selecting texts, curriculum, and tasks that push students beyond superficial facts to deeper understanding through immersion in reading, writing, thinking, and social practices. Teachers must be free to employ the tools, texts, and principles of their discipline to give students opportunities to *use* and *apply* knowledge, and that, in most middle and high schools, is a big order. But that big order *can* be handled by teachers who are expert in their disciplines and administrators who trust them to do their jobs.

Spotlight on Science

A large district joined others in adopting early release days where students are dismissed after half a day once a month to make time for teachers' professional development. Danita Hubert, physics teacher in a high school, decided to attend a workshop titled "Digging up Learning Through Questioning," since science is all about investigation. A few minutes into the presentation, Danita realized she needed the advanced course in questioning or, more likely, one targeted to the role of questioning in science. In physics, and in most of science in general, reading and reasoning are all based on asking the right questions, a skill Danita emphasizes from the first day students step into her class. "I teach kids to form questions in their heads at every stage of a problem: *Why? What happened? What is the difference? How do you know? What if?* The session I had chosen was about the importance of questioning—which I totally get—and a sort of formulaic approach to having kids learn to create good questions, a procedure that was better suited to history than to physics."

Danita's observation is vitally important with regard to disciplinary literacy. Formulating questions you want to ask the writer of an op-ed piece is a very different process from asking questions in a physics class; for example, *Why do heavier objects fall more quickly than light objects?* and then finding the answer through still more questions.

Perhaps Danita's valuable professional development time could have been better spent talking with her colleagues about how they lead students through investigations by asking pertinent questions or by reading and discussing with peers *How Students Learn: Science in the Classroom* (Donovan & Bransford, 2005). It's not that cross-disciplinary professional learning isn't important at times; it's just that focusing on issues inherent to the processes and content of a specific discipline can be a more efficient way of learning what works in your discipline—and what doesn't.

Disciplinary Reading, Writing, Inquiry, and Collaboration

In this volume, you will find four large chapters bookended by two smaller ones. Admittedly, each of the four major chapters could be a mini-book unto itself—reading, writing, inquiry, and collaboration—as these practices build the foundation of learning in every discipline. I present the chapters as springboards for disciplinary thinking as these components often have been neglected by teachers unable to differentiate and subsequently reclaim their content due in part to one-size-fits-all strategies, scripted programs, across-curriculum mandates, and fidelity to the textbook.

Now, at last, we have an approach to literacy that makes sense. One that teachers can use to *engage* students in the many dimensions of their disciplines. Read this book with a skeptical eye—just as we want all readers to approach text—and use or adapt the ideas, suggestions, activities and research to regain your content—and, perhaps, even your own teaching lives.

Suggestions for Further Reading

"Addressing Disciplinary Literacy in the Common Core Standards" by Michael Manderino and Corrine Wickens, 2014.

Adolescent Literacy in the Academic Disciplines: General Principles and Practical Strategies by Tamara L. Jetton and Cynthia Shanahan, 2012.

Content Matters: A Disciplinary Literacy Approach to Improving Student Learning by Stephanie M. McConachie and Anthony R. Petrosky (Eds.), 2010.

Deeper Learning: Beyond 21st Century Skills by James A. Bellanca (Ed.), 2015.

Disciplinary Literacy: Why It Matters and What You Should Do About It by Elizabeth Birr Moje, 2010. Available at https://www.youtube.com/watch?v=Id4gKJ-wGzU

Envisioning Knowledge: Building Literacy in the Academic Disciplines by Judith A. Langer, 2011.

Literacies of Discipline [Policy brief] by National Council of Teachers of English, 2011.

"Using the Common Core State Standards to Support Disciplinary Literacies" by Roni Jo Draper, March 2015.

Making it Relevant

1. How would you define literacy in your discipline?

2. What does deeper learning look like in your discipline? How about rigor?

3. If you had to name *the* most important skill students need in your discipline, what would that be? How does it compare to skills they may need in other subjects?

4. What has been your approach to literacy learning within your discipline in the past? What works? What would you like to change?

Notes:

2

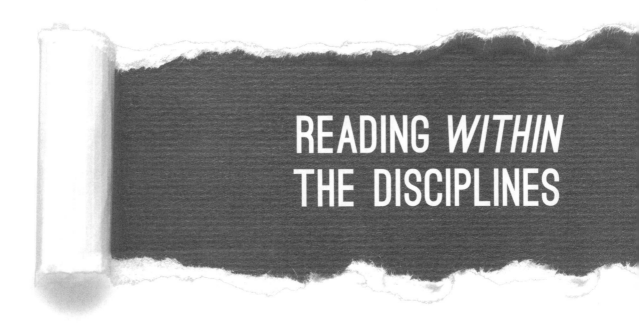

READING *WITHIN* THE DISCIPLINES

My husband is a scientist, and what I have learned in my many years of living with him is that his literacy practices and general interests revolve around a particular field of environmental and biological science. Our house is populated with journals, articles, and books about topics that I often consider to be strange, such as those on soil and earthworms, wooly adelgids, mammal skulls, and, perhaps not so strange, outrage over the damage humans have inflicted upon the earth. He is well educated and literate, but I have no doubt that he would quickly decline if someone asked him to speak to a group about reading or writing, insisting that questions be directed to me, the "literacy expert." But here's the catch. I'm no scientist, and while I could talk all day about how to use writing and reading in science, I could not show students how scientists use literacy to create meaning, analyze data, or write reports nearly as well as he could simply because *he* is the science expert and has been immersed in scientific literacy most of his life. Asking a science teacher to become a "teacher of reading" is not fair, nor is it an efficient use of her time. Instead, we must ask disciplinary teachers to share the secrets of literacy that work in their content areas.

The Benefits of Reading Within the Disciplines

Most content-area teachers read a lot: publications from professional organizations such as *Archaeological Conservancy*, popular discipline-specific periodicals like *Scientific American* or *Smithsonian*, or scholarly journals such as the *Quarterly Journal of Mathematics*. Books abound related to the disciplines as well: *The Immortal Life of Henrietta Lacks*, a true story about cells used in scientific research, or Nathaniel Philbrick's historical accounts of the *Mayflower* or Bunker Hill, for example. It goes without saying that most English language arts (ELA) teachers spend a good deal of their free time engaged in all sorts of reading. Though all these teachers use well-honed literacy skills to read very challenging text in their disciplines, they may not know how to *teach students* to use these same skills to access content; in fact, many teachers merely disseminate the content in the form of lectures or slide presentations and then test students on the information that has been transmitted.

As noted in the Chapter 1, the new focus on disciplinary literacy goes beyond reading strategies, which are generic in nature and aim to help the student comprehend general text. Disciplinary literacy is grounded in inquiry and emphasizes how students use the knowledge they are learning as a tool to participate in work within that discipline (Shanahan & Shanahan, 2012). So reading within a discipline doesn't mean simply "unlocking" the text or answering questions related to comprehension. It means that students understand how purpose and context inform their reading and that the act of reading can differ depending upon the text.

Asking a science teacher to become a "teacher of reading" is not fair, nor is it an efficient use of her time. Instead, we must ask disciplinary teachers to share the secrets of literacy that work in their content areas.

Shifts for Teaching Reading Within the Disciplines

- Rely less on generic reading strategies and more on discipline-specific literacy practices.

- Show students how experts in your field read relevant texts, not just how to read a textbook.

- Provide students with a wide variety of texts of varying lengths related to disciplinary topics instead of relying on a single resource.

- Model the language of the discipline by reading aloud and explaining why experts use words or terms in certain ways rather than engaging in isolated vocabulary study.

- Challenge students' perceptions of literacy by talking about how disciplinary experts read, write, speak, and think that might not conform to conventional rules in English language arts classes.

- Think in terms of how students will use new information to do work within the disciplines rather than only for test-taking purposes.

- Give students time to read in class and encourage reading at home.

Shifts for Reading Within the Disciplines

When considering disciplinary literacy, content-area teachers may do well to think in terms of shifts or changes in practice. What might such shifts look like? Take a look at the shaded box on this page.

The boxed list is certainly not exhaustive; two or more colleagues from the same discipline could create a much more relevant list for their subject if they were given the time and space to explore literacy in their subject areas. A middle school band director, for example, became concerned when he was told that all students in the school should read and write in every class. He approached the instructional coach and asked how he could incorporate literacy when he only had students thirty minutes every other day. "What should they be reading and writing?" he asked, followed by a long sigh. "How will I ever prepare them for their performance if they spend time reading instead of practicing?"

Good question, the reading coach acknowledged. They then began discussing musical literacy, the type of literacy that is necessary to "read" and, furthermore, "do" music as they identified texts as musical scores and even instruments. The longer they talked, the more the band director became enthusiastic about making literacy relevant to his content. Though print would not be the primary text in his discipline, he decided to ask the librarian to collect a set of books related to music for his students, and the coach suggested he share pertinent articles, websites, and musical reviews to demonstrate a real-world connection. "Maybe the kids could bring in articles as well to share or post on the bulletin board. I'm not sure they would like the reviews of classical music that I read," he laughed. The coach told me later that he was also having students write reflections of their musical experiences. A disciplinary literacy success story indeed.

What about reading in other academic areas? Sure, there are commonalities among the disciplines, but there are also striking differences. Let's begin with science.

Reading Within Science

Science is a discipline of inquiry, but in order to gain the content knowledge necessary for inquiry, students must use their reading skills to build knowledge. Unfortunately, science textbooks are sometimes very challenging for students due, in part, to superficially defined vocabulary and poorly written content. Such textbooks often douse natural curiosity regarding phenomena that are infinitely engaging. A child who fell in love with science in elementary school as she dissected an owl pellet to discover what lurked within complained later about having to take biology in high school. What happened? Perhaps too much emphasis in secondary classrooms has been placed on science as a topic to be studied instead of science as a process of exploration and discovery.

But even when students study scientific concepts through printed texts, the reading should be active.

Perhaps too much emphasis in secondary classrooms has been placed on science as a topic to be studied instead of science as a process of exploration and discovery.

How Do Scientists Read?

When scientists read, they

- Assume an objective stance
- Search for answers to relevant questions
- Sift through and evaluate quality and quantity of evidence
- Look for data-based outcomes
- Determine validity of source
- Decipher vocabulary necessary for conceptual understanding
- Question reasoning and conclusions
- Pay attention to detail and numbers
- Collaborate with colleagues when faced with complex ideas
- Chart, illustrate, and graph data and conclusions
- Consider alternatives to what has been presented
- Ask "Why?" more than "What?"
- Understand that theories are subject to change and seek out more current findings

Since science is often a social discipline, students should work within their peer scientific community to jigsaw material, exchange findings, and discuss ideas from their reading in an effort to understand new information or apply it through demonstrations, experiments, or reports. See Chapter 5 for more ideas related to collaborative learning.

Reading Within Math

One of the casualties of the "reading across the curriculum" movement has been the disenfranchisement of math teachers who felt they had to incorporate ELA reading into their classes. They often looked for stories and articles that were related to math, even tangentially, so they could meet the directive to become a "teacher of reading." Just as with the earlier example of the band director, we should have been asking math

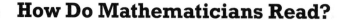

How Do Mathematicians Read?

When mathematicians read, they

- Use the information they are reading as pieces of a puzzle to be solved
- Make meaning out of mathematical symbols and abstract ideas
- Act as investigators looking for patterns and relationships
- Seek to understand what the problem is asking them to do rather than reading only for information
- Ask questions as they read
- Make notes of misconceptions or confusion
- Read for accuracy and clear mathematical reasoning
- Scrutinize ways that math is reported in the media or in real-world applications
- Apply previously learned mathematical concepts
- Look for what is missing
- Think about how vocabulary may be used differently in math contexts

Not only do mathematicians read differently than those in other disciplines, but they use what they are reading in different ways.

teachers what literacy looked like within their discipline. If we had asked, we may have been told that that mathematical literacy involves patterns, relationships, and examples of understanding through visuals or abstract representations. Not only do mathematicians read differently than those in other disciplines, but they use what they are reading in different ways.

In short, math is a discipline based on developing understanding through the act of solving problems, and the text often utilizes organization, language, and syntax that differ substantially from text in other disciplines.

Students of math need to come to text with an entirely different set of skills than students of English, history, or science, and math teachers should be free to show students just how these ways of reading differ.

Reading Within History and Social Studies

Close reading, the new buzzword in education, means that students attend to the text with a critical eye, perhaps reading more deeply than in the past. For social studies, close reading involves a variety of skills that are specific to the discipline, such as understanding how perspective may alter a historical account or how the context of a primary source document may change its meaning. Students must often deal with obsolete words in historical documents or unfamiliar terms and global contexts, making the reading especially challenging.

History can be complicated as it is both a science that begs for accuracy and a narrative dealing with the imperfect recollections and understandings of people who often can no longer be questioned. Furthermore, when students read in history, the required skills change with the event or account, so the complexity in reading within this discipline demands practice and awareness.

How Do Historians and Social Scientists Read?

When historians and social scientists read, they

- Compare and contrast events, accounts, documents, and visuals such as infographics or photographs
- Interpret primary and secondary sources with an eye toward bias
- Create narratives from existing information
- Use knowledge of the present to make sense of the past and vice versa
- Situate new understandings within background knowledge
- Think sequentially to piece together timelines
- Make inferences and determine what is important from what is merely interesting
- Untangle threads of fact from often conflicting accounts and perspectives
- Determine meanings of words within context

Reading Within ELA

Many believe that it is the job of the ELA teacher to teach students to read; however, English teachers are responsible for a curriculum that involves reading literature and, increasingly, informational text across multiple genres and through different lenses (e.g., cultural, historical, feminist). Reading novels, shorts stories, and poetry requires a mindset very different from that of readers of other disciplines—one that can recognize wordplay, hold on to multiple story lines, detect nuances in dialogue, and recognize how figurative language can expand meaning, for instance. Critical analysis of essays, articles, speeches, and other nonfiction texts require still a different set of skills. ELA teachers have their hands full, and they—just like every other content-area teacher—hope their students come to them already knowing how to read so they don't need to take on the role of "teacher of reading."

How Do Readers of Fiction and Nonfiction Approach Text?

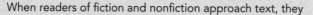

When readers of fiction and nonfiction approach text, they

- Look for ways that characters, setting, and conflicts may influence the meaning of the text
- Understand the use and effect of figurative language
- Find underlying messages that evolve as a theme
- Read skeptically, discerning unreliable narrators or characters
- Recognize devices authors use to enhance their writing, such as flashback, hyperbole, or analogy
- Read nonfiction critically, looking for bias or fallacies in reasoning
- Summarize and synthesize ideas in nonfiction and events in fiction
- Use reading as a way to make connections or understand real-world issues
- Understand how voice works to construct meaning
- Use text structure as a tool for comprehension
- Pay attention to new vocabulary or how words are used in unusual ways
- Engage in a mental dialogue with the author

Spotlight on ELA

English teacher Katherine Schmitt found a way to provide an authentic audience for her students' writing while generating a buzz about reading. "I had my freshman students create 'shelf talkers' for our library. Students selected books that they would recommend to others. They then wrote a brief description of the book and explained why the book is worth reading. I had the librarians go over the reviews to make sure the shelf talkers were suitable for posting in the library. Then, the library staff put the students' reviews next to the books the students had recommended. The kids were really excited to see their writing out in public and took great joy in showing other people what they wrote."

Stephanie Weiss and Jolene Heinemann teach in a large school and don't have their own rooms so maintaining a classroom library is difficult. Based on an idea they heard about from Shana Karnes at a National Council of Teachers of English (NCTE) session, they created a digital library with creative shelf titles that would guide students to their "bookmate." "We also wanted to get students intrinsically interested in researching, finding, and trying out new books," said Stephanie. They sorted popular books into student-friendly genres like Books for the Beach, Are You Afraid of the Dark? Fight to Survive, Rough Stuff, and so forth. "We use color-coding to designate which books are in the English office or in a specific classroom so students know where to go to sign them out," Stephanie explains. The digital library also includes elements that a physical library doesn't, like links to the Barnes & Noble book descriptions. Best of all, "Students participate by giving book talks. We add their recommendations to a page titled, appropriately, Student Recommendations."

Katherine Schmitt's students write "shelf talkers" for books in the school library to encourage other students to take a look at their favorites.

When reading in ELA is combined with reading in other disciplines, students have opportunities to develop a well-rounded approach to a variety of texts, but let's be clear: English teachers should not be expected to teach students how to read in every discipline any more than math teachers should be expected to teach students how to read *War and Peace*.

English teachers should not be expected to teach students how to read in every discipline any more than math teachers should be expected to teach students how to read War and Peace.

Questions (and Answers) About Reading Within the Disciplines

There's a big movement at my school for "wide and rigorous reading." Why am I, a content-area teacher, responsible for students' "wide" reading?

Just as we will see with writing, inquiry, and collaboration, reading in the disciplines is a tool to support content-area study, a means for moving students not only toward understanding but also toward independence. Take a look at how time spent reading increases students' word exposure in Figure 2.1, for instance.

We also know that students who read more have distinct academic advantages over students who read less—and they do better in content-area studies as well. Not surprisingly, students' reading achievement and overall success in school correlates positively to the amount of independent reading they do (Anderson, Wilson, & Fielding, 1988; Greaney, 1980). The introduction to an important study on reading from the National Endowment for the Arts, *To Read or Not to Read* (2007), states the facts quite clearly: "The habit of daily reading . . . overwhelmingly correlates with better reading skills and higher academic achievement. On the other hand, poor reading skills correlate with lower levels of financial and job success" (pp. 5–6).

It only makes sense that students should be reading *something* in every class every day related to the content, ideally something so interesting that they will want to continue reading outside of class. Once students

Figure 2.1

Independent Reading Adds Up to Significant Word Exposure

INDEPENDENT READING	
Minutes per Day	Words per Year
65	4,358,000
21.1	1,823,000
14.2	1,146,000
6.5	432,000
1.3	106,000

Source: Adapted from Anderson, Wilson, & Fielding, 1998.

turn into readers, they *will* read widely. As a content-area teacher, you should make engaging, disciplinary-relevant texts available to your students and give them time to read.

I have a personal story regarding this question. Early in my career as a high school teacher, I had the freedom and funding to buy subscriptions of class sets of *Time* magazines. With my co-teacher, an American government and economics teacher, we would assign several articles to students, and when the lesson was complete, they were free to take the magazines home and read articles on their own, often sharing what they had read with parents. Students' test scores, engagement, and reading skills soared with this practice. Years later, many students contacted us to tell us that the habit they had developed of reading current events in high school helped them succeed in college and sparked an interest

As a content-area teacher, you should make engaging, disciplinary-relevant texts available to your students, and give them time to read.

Nicolas Yeager

In Nicolas Yeager's senior English class, students read independently, but he also asks them to read seventeen minutes a day outside of class, which adds up to two hours a week, a significant increase over their reading time in previous years.

that stayed with them into adulthood. It wasn't necessarily our job to get students reading widely, but we (and they) enjoyed tremendous advantages when we did.

My students are required to read from the textbook. Isn't that enough?

Many students have become quite proficient at skimming or fake-reading just to pinpoint answers to textbook questions. Even if students read entire chapters from textbooks, however, they may not gain the advantages of wide reading described above. In researching various textbooks for *Overcoming Textbook Fatigue* (Lent, 2012), I found textbook writing often dull, at times even inconsiderate, textbook vocabulary defined but not conceptualized, and textbook topics often covered so superficially that students became overwhelmed rather than informed. In addition, textbooks often included stale or incorrect information. But the real issue is that we no longer gain all of the information available on a topic through a single source. Without going into a diatribe against textbooks, suffice it to say that students need exposure to many types of print and digital texts to meet the challenges of college, career, and a literate life.

One of the easiest ways to meet those challenges is to flood students with reading within your disciplines. "But what should students read besides the textbook?" teachers often ask as they ponder the impossibility of finding time to incorporate even more into an already overwhelming curriculum. "And how do I get students reading anything at all, much less the textbook?" We may all agree that kids should be reading more, but making that happen may be one of the most challenging tasks teachers face in every grade and every discipline. Let's move to the next question to address that topic.

Figure 2.2

What Should Students Read in Content-Area Classes?

- Websites, blogs
- Fiction and nonfiction, including historical and science fiction, graphic novels and comics
- Timelines
- Journals and magazines with sections, features or entire articles related to the topic of study
- Current events, news briefs, headlines
- Word problems
- Narratives
- Parts of the whole: chapters in handbooks and manuals, lists, one of a series of articles, sections of textbooks or nonfiction
- Primary documents: letters, journals, lyrics, newspaper reports, posters, ethnographic notes, historical accounts, transcripts, court records, travelogues, maps
- Visual text: infographics, cartoons, illustrations, photographs, diagrams, signs
- Raw data, lab or field notes, journals
- Tables, graphs
- Personal communication: letters, emails, texts, tweets, interviews,
- Multimodal texts
- Advertisements

I have students of varying reading abilities in my class, many of whom can't or won't read, and I have pretty much given up on having them read even the textbook. How do I engage my students in reading anything at all?

The quickest way to help students develop reading habits in your discipline is to give students a choice of texts on the same topic at various reading levels. Many studies, most significantly John Guthrie's (2007) work on adolescents' engagement in literacy, have found that students who are most engaged in reading are those who are allowed to shape their own reading through autonomy and ownership.

Let's say you are deep into a unit on the civil rights movement in social studies with Rosa Parks as the topic of study. You can find hundreds of resources about her, from articles to a blogs to books of nonfiction. Allow students to find the text they want to read, which in itself will reduce resistance, or give them a choice from several options.

Once they have entered the topic through a text of their own choosing, offer a more challenging text, perhaps an article you want the entire class to read—but mix it up to keep engagement high. Some days you could read just a few paragraphs of a more complex text such as a recent piece from the *New York Times* about Claudette Colvin, a teenager who refused to give up her seat on a segregated bus prior to Parks' act of civil disobedience, and then have kids read the rest of the text on their own. Other days, you may want to place a paragraph of complex text on the screen and read with students, deconstructing as you read; other days, you may give students text that they will partner-read, and still other days their reading may not involve much more than a few lines of text on a political cartoon or infographic.

Most important, make the reading as active as possible by having kids stop and talk after reading a few paragraphs or write questions in their learning logs as they read. See page 82 for more information on learning logs.

The idea isn't that the entire class read the same amount of text or the same text each day; it's that they read *something* and, in the process, learn the essential skills of finding, evaluating, and applying what they are reading.

The idea isn't that the entire class read the same amount of text or the same text each day; it's that they read something.

Spotlight on Special Education

Carlynn Ullrich Sherman, ELA teacher, describes how she uses a text set to provide background and motivation before having her students read *The Call of the Wild:*

> I used the jigsaw method to introduce *The Call of the Wild* by Jack London to a group of 8th graders in an instructional (special education) setting. The students read at grade level for the most part, but tend to get frustrated with new topics, especially if there is little background knowledge. I had students break up into small groups and choose an informational text from several that I had gathered from a variety of sources:
>
> - A screen shot of the weather in the Yukon Territory provided by the Government of Canada for the month of December
> - A primary document of the Yukon/Klondike Gold Rush stampeders' supply list, 1898
> - An article about the role women played in the gold rush from the Library of Congress
> - Several photos with captions of people in the Gold Rush
> - An article about the California Gold Rush taken from http://www.u-s-history.com
>
> The jigsaw task asks students to evaluate author credibility, choose quotes (evidence) to support a claim, create questions they may have, and write an unbiased summary. In small groups, students addressed the task through discussion and then wrote their answers on a piece of posterboard. After completing the activity, students presented to the class their findings.
>
> During the students' presentations, I projected a "teaser picture" of each article on the Smartboard so the audience could have a visual connection with what the students were saying. Not only did this lesson touch on reading informational text and writing goals for eighth graders, but speaking and listening got a slam dunk, as well.

Yukon/Klondike
Gold Rush
Stampeder's Supply List, 1898

Every person traveling to the goldfields of the Yukon Territory were required to take along one year's worth of supplies. Every dealer of goods was ready to tell them exactly what they needed, and would sell the products to them at a very high price. There were also many how-to books for the prospector. Many were written by people that were never in the wilderness, let alone the Yukon.

List of items needed by miners distributed by the Northern Pacific Railroad:

For each man:

FOOD:

200 pounds of bacon
400 pounds of flour
85 pounds assorted dried fruit
50 pounds cornmeal
35 pounds rice
24 pounds coffee
5 pounds tea
100 pounds sugar
25 pounds fish
15 pounds soup vegetables
50 pounds oatmeal
50 pounds dried potatoes
50 pounds dried onions
25 cans butter
100 pounds beans
4 dozen tins condensed milk
15 pounds salt
1 pound pepper
8 pounds baking powder
2 pounds baking soda
½ pound mustard
¾ pound ginger
36 pounds yeast cakes
60 boxes of matches

CLOTHING:

1 suit oil clothing
3 pairs snag-proof rubber boots
3 pairs heavy shoes
1 dozen heavy socks
6 pairs wool mittens
3 suits heavy underwear
2 pairs Mackinaw trousers
2 pairs overalls
2 hats
4 heavy woolen overshirts
1 Mackinaw coat
1 heavy rubber-lined coat
suspenders, handkerchiefs, snow glasses
2 pairs of heavy woolen blankets
2 oil blankets
4 towels
buttons, thread, needles
5 yards mosquito netting

Students in Carlynn Ullrich Sherman's class were especially interested in the supplies that Gold Rush stampeders were expected to bring along with them. "200 pounds of bacon?" one student asked incredulously while others in the group voiced their surprise at the quantity of other items before deciding on how they would present the information to the rest of the class.

Getting kids to read every day sounds great in a perfect world, but I hardly have enough time to plan lessons. How will I find the time to select texts for students to read each day, especially if they aren't all reading the same text?

I won't pretend that being a text scout is easy, but I can say with certainty that it is a lot more satisfying than plowing through the teacher's edition of your textbook. Actually, finding texts can be an integral part of the time you spend planning lessons (unless you are, in fact, going lockstep through the textbook, which would be unfortunate). It's really a matter of how you think about texts. As you read for your own enjoyment or edification, think in terms of your students. If you find something online or in a journal that relates to your discipline, share it with students—even if you give them only a part of the whole text to read.

In addition, one of the most important (and enjoyable) tasks of a professional learning community (PLC) is to take on the role of text scavenger, always on the lookout for texts that can be shared with students as they study specific units. By the way, creating activities that enhance lessons are a much more productive use of a PLC's time than addressing logistical or management issues. Create a Google Doc space or a physical place to store texts related to various topics in your discipline until needed. Better yet, ask students to help you find articles, websites, or blogs relevant to units. Assign students dates they will be responsible for providing quick reads for the class related to the topic of study. The advantages of such a practice are obvious: Students are reading more, evaluating text for a "real" audience, and taking ownership of their own learning.

Don't forget to include your librarian in your search as well. Most are eager to find texts on various topics and many schools subscribe to online resource services that you might not be aware of, so ask for help and then share the bounty.

My instructional coach talks about Lexiles and challenging text. How am I supposed to know the Lexile of a supplemental text or if a particular text is challenging enough for my students?

For the purpose of increasing the volume of reading related to your discipline, don't worry about Lexiles or the readability levels of texts.

Think in terms of content. Will the ideas in the text increase your students' understanding of concepts, challenge them think in new ways, or broaden their background knowledge? If so, the text fulfills a pedagogical purpose despite its Lexile. Think about wide and frequent reading as foundational for the more difficult reading that students will be required to do in your course.

Having said that, I know that many schools use "Lexile language" as part of the growth metric or to ensure that students are being challenged. An ELA teacher told me recently that she uses Lexiles for "book reports" but not for independent reading, and I remember thinking that some of the books her students are reading independently may be far more difficult conceptually than the ones in their designated Lexile.

My concern with Lexiles is that they are often not reliable and can harm the reading habits of kids who are forced to stay within a "range" of bands. *Night,* for example, falls into the Lexile range of 570, but anyone who has read the book knows that this autobiographical account of Elie Wiesel's horrifying experience in the Nazi death camps is tough reading for anyone, much less a third or fourth grader. I could give many examples of such faulty Lexiles, so I always encourage teachers to consider the content of the text and how it relates to their topic before looking at Lexile. I agree with the high school librarian who said, "I've seen students read books and articles way above their Lexile when they are motivated to do so and others who are not allowed to engage in a book that would definitely challenge them because it is 'ranged' below their Lexile. It doesn't make sense to me."

I often call on different students to read out loud as a way of making sure they are paying attention. Is this a good idea?

Round-robin reading, the practice of having one student at a time read a paragraph or calling on students to read, turns the act of reading, something which should be an inherently satisfying activity, into a guessing game. Furthermore, the anxiety associated with such a practice, especially for struggling or shy readers, creates an environment that makes comprehension difficult, if not impossible. It is far preferable to allow students to read aloud with another student (called *paired reading*), though this activity can turn up the volume exponentially in a classroom.

We want students to have plenty of practice reading silently, as well, since that is generally how most adults read for pleasure or information. Try to find ways of engaging students in reading by building background, tapping into curiosity, creating relevance, or having them read a short section and "turn and talk" to a partner or small group rather than artificially keeping them on task by making them wonder if they will be the next one on the reading hot seat.

How will I know kids are really reading text I've assigned without giving them a quiz every day?

While quizzes have their place, we all know that such assessments can be flawed, especially when a student has read the text but misses one question out of, say, five, which would give the student a barely passing score. More significantly, quizzing students after reading sends the message that reading is not inherently interesting or valuable and must be constantly monitored. Often, kids feel that once the quiz is finished the task is complete, relegating reading to a chore to be completed for someone else rather than an intrinsically satisfying (and necessary) life skill.

I am concerned with computerized reading quizzes for this same reason. The questions on such quizzes often fail to get at deep ideas in a text and tend to be formatted for easy computer scoring instead of eliciting thoughtful answers from students. And quizzes tied to reading programs that seek to increase the volume of students' reading often create a sort of reading race where students try to become the winner in a contest that often has more to do with competition than with the cerebral act of reading. It is far better for a student to become deeply engaged with reading one book that may stay with her for life than to be able to answer questions about multiple books that she may have merely skimmed so she could pass a quiz.

In fact, not all kids will read with equal passion or interest each day, and that's OK. Instead of a giving a quiz, wander around the room talking with students about what they are reading and encourage discussion after reading. If necessary, give participation grades or ask students to respond to what they have read, but avoid the low-level comprehension questions that are typical of most quizzes. As an aside, in a class where kids are busy doing the work of the discipline instead of always reading about it, quizzes aren't necessary because the teacher can evaluate students' understandings through more authentic measures, such as presentations, demonstrations, or models of learning.

Should supplemental reading always be related to the topic of study?

While it may seem that you are off topic if you provide texts that aren't directly tied to your current topic of study, any text from your subject area helps broaden understanding of your discipline overall. Increasingly, the world is not divided into isolated components of information but rather consists of a smorgasbord of knowledge, often related in tangential ways. If you are teaching cell division, for example, providing an article about the Ebola epidemic can expand understanding and provide valuable insight into the world. Similarly, having math students read an article from the *New York Times* about a robotics exhibit at the national Museum of Mathematics based on changing algorithms can provide increased understanding of or curiosity about mathematical patterns that may provide students with a foundation for other mathematical concepts.

We've had a ton of in-service on reading strategies for years in my school, and I've tried them all, but my students seem to have real difficulties simply reading. Maybe reading strategies aren't the answer after all?

While there are some strategies that help students comprehend better in all disciplines, such as K-W-L (what I know, what I want to know, what I learned) or variations of this practice, not all strategies are a perfect match for all disciplines. Cynthia Shanahan, a reading researcher, writes about a student who was not doing well in science because he was "reading for the gist," a strategy that may be useful in history but a disaster for reading science, where every detail and technical term is important (Shanahan & Shanahan, 2012). Similarly, certain graphic organizers work better for some subjects and topics than others. Students should learn to use strategies as metacognitive tools to help them comprehend—just as we use any tool that will help us get the job done. Show students a variety of strategies that work with your content and encourage them to choose the ones they need to use when appropriate.

As for helping students who have real difficulty with reading, make sure you contact the reading teacher or reading specialist just in case these kids have fallen between the cracks in terms of intervention. I contend that

Students will never become better readers by filling in worksheets, memorizing steps in strategies, or reading only to answer questions. Readers are created when they engage in the practice of reading.

many students want us to believe they can't read when, in fact, they simply don't want to read or have had so little practice reading that they have come to believe they aren't readers. Such behavior is called *aliteracy*, but fortunately it's not terminal. When provided with engaging texts, "reluctant" students often prove they can read pretty well. In any case, give such students opportunities to partner-read or work in groups with other students as a way to get them actively reading. Remember that you are responsible for helping students learn to read content in your discipline, not teaching them to read overall, and that always means providing a wide variety of texts in your content area. Students will never become better readers by filling in worksheets, memorizing steps in strategies, or reading only to answer questions.

Readers are created when they engage in the practice of reading.

How to Get Students Reading in Every Discipline Every Day

1. CURRENT EVENTS SHORT TAKES: MAKING DISCIPLINARY LEARNING RELEVANT

Nicolas Yeager

Diego has read thirteen books this year because he is in a class where his teacher provides time for students to read. Diego said, "The more you read, the better your literacy gets. Reading can also change your perspective on the world. What I thought I fully understood about the world, I've come to understand differently since I've begun reading."

Content-area teachers know which sites offer the most accurate and in-depth information for their discipline, but they sometimes think they don't have time to incorporate current events, even those related their content. I argue that we *must* incorporate news pieces in all subject areas if we want students to make the necessary connections for deeper learning and more challenging tasks.

The key to this activity is providing relevant current events on a regular basis to increase relevance, interest, and learning. Both print periodicals and reputable online sources provide the latest articles, charts, graphs, lists, photographs, research, and even word problems. In case you missed it, the *New York Times* reported on a math problem from Singapore, "When is Cheryl's birthday?" that went viral. Check it out at www .nytimes.com/2015/04/15/science/a-math-problem-from-singapore-goes-viral-when-is-cheryls-birthday.html. The *Huffington Post* provided the answer in an article at www.huffingtonpost.com/2015/04/15/cheryls-birthday-answer_n_7067790.html. Math and current events, what a great combination!

How It Works

Let's look at how a short piece of online news supports the disciplinary literacy skills we want students to learn and use.

A quick search of "history news" leads me to discovery.com's history site. As I scan the headlines, I am interested in a story with the headline: *Roman Gladiators Drank Ash Energy Drink* because I know lots of students who practically live on energy drinks. I read the article and am surprised to find that Roman gladiators' diets were very different from the high protein diet of current athletes. Roman gladiators primarily ate wheat, barley, and beans—but not much dairy (news.discovery.com/history/archaeology/roman-gladiators-drank-ash-energy-drink-141027.htm discover.com). I thought I was reading a history article, but I soon learned the content was more science than history, specifically regarding the minerals that are found in bones. I learned more than I expected from a 360-word article, but that is only the beginning.

I clicked on *The Coolest Archeological Discoveries of 2014*. I thought it might be interesting to give students one of these discoveries a day, starting with an article about a shipwreck found under the World Trade Center or maybe the one about a teenager in a black hole. It's true that some teachers might decide not to provide the article on King Tut's 3,300-year erection, but when students discover this article on their own, they will increase their vocabulary exposure by 200 words, including content-specific words such as *monotheism* and *polytheism*. They will also tap into a bit of mythology, a reference to Osiris, the Egyptian god of the underworld, who is often depicted with an erect penis to evoke his regenerative powers. While they are at it, students may click on other links about the new findings regarding King Tut based on a recent reconstruction and read precisely the type

Tips for Using Current Event Short Takes

Sometimes short takes unrelated to the day's lesson work by themselves, but other current events are perfect for specific curriculum topics. The riots and marches in major American cities during the summer of 2014 because of the failure of the grand jury to indict a white police officer in the death of African American Michael Brown offer a current context for Martin Luther King's (1963) "I Have a Dream" speech or Sharon Draper's 2008 novel, *Fire From the Rock,* for example. There are countless way to incorporate current events short takes into any lesson.

- Provide short texts to begin class each day, perhaps with a turn-and-talk question to end the reading.
- Use the texts to "prime the pump" or as an introduction to the lesson.
- Create reading breaks with short takes to encourage engagement and recapture attention.
- Provide links to articles that students can choose to read on devices during independent reading time or if they finish an assignment early.
- Place students in small groups and have one group member each day responsible for providing a current event short take. If time permits, allow students to engage in discussion between groups.
- Choose a longer article or an article with parts (such as a list article) and have students read one part of it each day, concluding with some sort of corresponding activity, such as a debate, WebQuest, or writing assignment.
- Provide an article each week for everyone in the school or your class to read, such as an article about Malala Yousafzai when she won the Nobel Peace Prize in 2014. Find one that is a bit more challenging than "just the facts" articles to encourage sustained reading. An article from the *New York Times* titled "Taliban Gun Down Girl Who Spoke Up for Rights" is an example of just such a text. Access it at www.nytimes.com/2012/10/10/world/asia/teen-school-activist-malala-yousafzai-survives-hit-by-pakistani-taliban.html.
- Use the Smithsonian Tween Tribune site (tweentribune.com) for quality nonfiction related to science, social studies, ELA, and math.

of complex text we want them to read. Look at how the following short paragraph provides examples of argumentation, corroborating evidence, and sophisticated syntax all embedded in a short but engaging text.

Previous theories suggested King Tut may have died as a result of a chariot accident, but a virtual reconstruction showed a different scenario. "It was important to look at his ability to ride on a chariot and we concluded it would not be possible for him, especially with his partially clubbed foot, as he was unable to stand unaided," Albert Zink, head of the Institute for Mummies and Icemen in Italy, told the U.K. daily *The Independent.* According to Ashraf Selim, an Egyptian radiologist, King Tut "also developed Kohler's disease or death of the bones, during adolescence, which would have been incredibly painful" (Lorenzi, 2014).

Why It Works

As students become more aware of the world around them and their place in it, they also tend to invite learning rather than perceiving it apart from their real lives.

As students become more aware of the world around them and their place in it, they also tend to invite learning rather than perceiving it apart from their real lives.

Give them an article about how McDonald's is revamping its menu toward more healthful options in consumer science, for example, and students just might pay attention to news reports regarding how fast food is contributing to obesity or the latest report that diet sodas actually lead to diabetes.

Current events can also create a cumulative, sometimes addictive, effect as events unfold. Mark Kelly, Gabrielle Gifford's astronaut husband, and his twin, Scott Kelly, also an astronaut, are involved in a groundbreaking study about how the body adapts to life in space as Scott spends over a year in space and Mark remains on earth. Keep students on top of these developments to encourage sustained reading about a single topic even if the topic doesn't fit with "today's lesson."

Extend and Adapt

Independent reading, the reading students choose to do on their own, can add up to significant increases in learning across the curriculum. A variety of studies show that students who read independently not only become better readers, but they score higher on achievement tests in all subject areas and have greater content knowledge than those who do not (Cunningham & Stanovich, 1991; Krashen, 1993; Stanovich & Cunningham, 1993). Jeffrey Wilhelm and

Michael W. Smith, authors of *Reading Unbound* (2013), reported on a series of sophisticated analyses that showed a positive link between independent reading and cognitive outcomes. Furthermore, pleasure reading was found to be three times more significant in contributing to a child's cognitive progress than was the parents' educational attainment. Independent reading, whether implemented schoolwide or within a single class, is clearly beneficial.

The key to this practice is allowing students to choose their reading, preferably from a well-stocked classroom library full of a wide variety of texts. Students should also have devices available where they can choose articles from websites. Some teachers allow students to read a set amount of time each day, especially in ELA classes where students may be reading novels. Many content teachers provide time on a weekly basis, say, fifteen or twenty minutes once or twice a week. While students should choose their own reading, the teacher can help them make good choices by promoting interesting texts to the class or making recommendations to individual students. As students read, teachers should wander about the room, checking in and using this opportunity for a bit of differentiated instruction. It's also a good idea to allow students to share what they are reading periodically to encourage engagement.

Spotlight on History and Social Studies

Contributed by Kurt Weisenburger and Robert Seidel, AP US history teachers

We utilize a course hashtag on Twitter as a medium to emphasize literacy while also teaching 21st century skills. Our continuous Twitter discussion demonstrates appropriate use of social networking while creating a positive online footprint—and allows students to share their ideas with a real audience that extends outside the classroom while connecting information with the current unit of study. Students

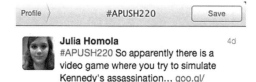

Julia Homola   4d
#APUSH220 So apparently there is a
video game where you try to simulate
Kennedy's assassination... goo.gl/
xGKWlk

Olivia Hagan   4d
Only 32% of people in a poll believe that
Oswald carried out the killing on his own
@TIME goo.gl/8POgU9 #APUSH220

Max Gersten   3/11/15
Another important figure of the 20s, FBI
director J. Edgar Hoover. Here, testing
out a "tommy"machine gun. #APUSH220

Twitter

Example of a Twitter feed created by students
in Kurt Weisenburger and Robert Seidel's
history classes.

share in-depth articles about topics of their own choosing, usually ones in which they are personally interested. Videos and visuals that go beyond our classroom are also popular contributions.

Students make connections between our course content and current events, sharing articles or opinions that demonstrate such relationships. Finally, students share personal items that give the course hashtag its own culture. This may include history-related jokes, photos, and personal experiences like vacations that contribute to a positive environment and further reinforce the idea that 21st century literacy is a continuous practice.

Our utilization of this technology also blends with the new AP US history curriculum, which emphasizes historical thinking skills and a more in-depth knowledge of fewer elements of content than the earlier version of the exam. The College Board no longer want students to know a little bit about a lot of content; they wants students to read more widely and deeply on selected areas. Our use of Twitter allows students to decide what topics they will read most widely, and then share their findings with their peers and the world. The new skill-based AP US history exam is also one that requires extensive reading abilities. The number one way to improve reading abilities is to read often, and our course hashtag encourages students to do just that while also empowering them with the ability to choose what they read.

2. READING ALOUD: A BRIDGE TO COMPLEX TEXT

With the emphasis on complex text within the disciplines, it is more important than ever for students of all ages to hear text being read aloud. I'm not suggesting that teachers read to students all period or read aloud in place of having students engage in silent reading, of course, but students need to hear how experts in the field communicate—especially when the text is too challenging for readers to access on their own.

Read aloud to students from any source that works within your discipline: journals, novels, nonfiction, blogs, or commentaries, for instance. And, don't think you need to be a professional reader to get students engaged in a piece of text. Generally, all you have to do is tell them you want to share something and demonstrate how it makes sense within your discipline. Tim Kramer, social studies teacher, says he often begins class by reading something aloud that he finds interesting, funny or well written. His students see how much pleasure his own reading brings to him and they begin to look for passages to share with the class as well.

How It Works

Take a look at one paragraph of an article a science teacher decided to use as a read-aloud from the January 2015 issue from *Scientific American* because it contains "all sorts of scientific concepts written in a scholarly manner that still engages." In it, the author describes how fish live in darkness and extreme cold below the ice in Antarctica, perhaps surviving on some type of chemical energy (http://www.nature.com/news/fish-live-beneath-antarctica-1.16772).

> Stunned researchers in Antarctica have discovered fish and other aquatic animals living in perpetual darkness and cold, beneath a roof of ice 740 metres thick. The animals inhabit a wedge of seawater only 10 metres deep, sealed between the ice above and a barren, rocky seafloor below—a location so remote and hostile the many scientists expected to find nothing but scant microbial life. (Fox, 2015)

Students who may not be able to read this article on their own will gain valuable understandings of biology and robotics by listening to it being read aloud. In addition, they are exposed to scientific vocabulary that demonstrates to them how science is communicated in the real world.

How to Read Aloud

- Read slowly and with as much showmanship as you possess to engage students in active listening.

- Sprinkle in your own thoughts about the content as you read, including how you monitor your comprehension. Pause to figure out confusing content when appropriate.

- Have students jot questions in their learning logs for later discussion or conduct a more active read-aloud with students raising hands to ask questions as you read.

- You may also stop periodically to ask questions regarding the content. In the earlier example, you might ask, "Do you know how thick 740 meters is?" or "What is an example of microbial life?"

- It's often helpful to model how you might disagree with the author or question facts or sources.

- If you decide to read the entire article aloud, stop often and have students turn and talk to deepen comprehension.

- Some teachers project visuals as they read such as accompanying photographs or illustrations from the article. You may provide a copy of the article either in print or projected on the screen so students can follow along as you read, but that step is not always necessary; sometimes just having students listen is enough.

- If the article is from an online source, provide the link so students can reread it if they are interested and point out related sites to encourage them to pursue new learning.

- Most of all, try not to turn a read-aloud into an assignment; instead, approach it as a bonus—something enjoyable that you can't wait to share.

Ideas for Reading Aloud

- Choose a novel such as Nancy Farmer's *House of Scorpion* (2004) for a science class and read to students the last five minutes of class each day. A novel that may appear to be written for younger children, Kate DiCamillo's *Tiger Rising* (2002), for example, contains examples of figurative language, allusion, and strong characterization, making it a perfect text to read aloud, a few pages at a time in an ELA class, to reinforce how literary devices are used to create effect. Christopher Jett wrote an entire article on how he engaged his math students with Wendy Lichtman's novel *Do the Math #1: Secrets, Lies, and Algebra* (2008). Unbelievably, students will turn into the children of their past, begging you to read or sitting perfectly still, listening as you seemingly cast a spell simply by reading aloud.

Students in Amy Suessen's social studies class listen intently as Amy supplements her lesson with a read-aloud.

- Read a particularly difficult text, such as a piece from the *New York Times* on immigration in social studies and explain to them how and why the writer is making word, structure, or other craft choices.

- Read a controversial piece to students such as Carl Hiaasen's op-ed piece on the death penalty, "Cruel and Unusual Ways of Execution," and ask students to consider the validity of his arguments. Often teachers feel that when introducing a commentary, they should create activities such as writing, discussion, or debate, but it is often enough to simply real the piece and leave it to simmer.

- Surprise students with an unexpected read-aloud, such as a poem by popular poet Billy Collins or a picture book related to your content, such as Peter Sis' *Starry Messenger: Galileo Galilei* (2000)—with amazing scientific illustrations— or Lemony Snicket's *The Composer Is Dead* (2009) in music class, complete with a CD.

Why It Works

Reading aloud provides opportunities for students to hear how a writer's voice can change a piece through the use of sarcasm or parody, for example, or how scientific or mathematical writing uses inquiry to engage in a process. In addition, many English language learners or students who have difficulty decoding are, nevertheless, plenty smart and anxious to learn. As they listen to text being read aloud, especially complex text, students gain content knowledge and become familiar with the cadence and prosody that comes naturally to proficient readers. In some cases, simply listening to complex text being read aloud helps reluctant students approach the text with more confidence.

Extend and Adapt

Many students are exceptional readers, especially those who already have a knack for the dramatic. Allow them to use their skills by asking them to read a short piece of text to the class or to partner-read an interview, for example. *Time* magazine offers a feature most weeks called "10 Questions" where they print interviews with subjects ranging from the daughter of a Nazi war criminal to major sports figures to humanitarians and economists. The interviews are short and often extremely engaging or thought provoking, such as a recent "10 Questions" with Judy Blume that include a question about why her children's books are often banned.

Consider having experts in the field choose texts to read aloud to students such as someone from the health department reading instructions for how to conduct a quarantine or an engineer showing how she might read blueprints. Actors from a local theater can provide compelling readings of literature in ELA classes, especially Shakespeare, and lawyers can often read texts regarding legal decisions, explaining complex language as they read.

3. GETTING IT VISUALLY: INFOGRAPHICS, CHARTS, GRAPHS, POLITICAL CARTOONS, PHOTOGRAPHS, AND ILLUSTRATIONS

In case anyone hasn't noticed, we are teaching a generation that loves visuals. Just because students are inundated with visuals doesn't mean they know how to read them, however. A novice high school math

As they listen to text being read aloud, especially complex text, students gain content knowledge and become familiar with the cadence and prosody that comes naturally to proficient readers.

teacher was astounded when she realized that her students were unable to critically evaluate a simple infographic. She found that they looked only at the images and generally accepted the message as credible.

So, providing more visuals to students may not be enough; we must help students learn to read visuals as they would any other text and understand how they are used to construct (or skew) meaning in each discipline. Students should also learn how to create strong visuals that convey accurate information.

How It Works

Project a visual text on the screen or provide a hard copy for students, either the same text or a different visual for each small group. Have students read and analyze the text using some or all of the questions in "Questions for Interpreting Visual Text." Explain to students that text, either in the form of words or images, communicates ideas by the author or creator that the reader must accurately interpret.

Providing more visuals to students may not be enough; we must help students learn to read visuals as they would any other text.

Questions for Interpreting Visual Text

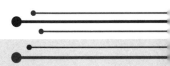

1. What do you see? How do you "read" the text?

2. What is the purpose of the visual?

3. What more do you need to know to fully understand the message of the text?

4. How could you find out what you need to know?

5. Is the source credible? How do you know?

6. Whose viewpoint is not represented?

7. Do you agree with the author's point? Why or why not?

8. How would you change the text to make it more understandable?

9. How would you summarize the information in the text?

10. Who would be most interested in the information presented in the text? Why?

Available for download at http://resources.corwin.com/lentDL

Ideas for Incorporating Visual Literacy

1. Cartoons are clever and engaging ways to help students learn how to read visuals. The science cartoon in Figure 2.3, for example, could be used by a science teacher when teaching a unit on the periodic table. Ask students to discuss the cartoon with their learning partner or write what they see happening in the cartoon and why.

2. Use picture books to focus students' attention on visuals. Aaron Becker's wordless picture book, *Journey* (2013), for example, compels students to rely on the illustrations to gain meaning from the story. Ask your librarian to help you find appropriate picture books to support your units. Some librarians have created sections in the professional libraries for storing picture books related to content-area topics that teachers can check out.

3. Have students bring in and exchange advertisements with a strong visual. They can then use the questions in "Questions for Interpreting Visual Text" to analyze the advertisement before creating their own ad containing both a compelling visual and a carefully worded message.

4. Find examples of visuals related to your content area in the real world or ask students to bring in examples.

5. Have students in social studies choose photographs from an era in history (the Library of Congress website at www.loc.gov/ has a nice collection) and write captions to accompany the images.

Why It Works

Visual literacy is important because we know that nonlinguistic representations of a concept, especially when paired with print, can increase students' ability to learn (Marzano, Pickering, & Pollock, 2001). Many students who have difficulty with print-centric text can find meaning from illustrations, graphs, diagrams, and other visuals, but they often need guidance in deciphering such text accurately. Conversely, students who are good readers may have difficulty with visual text. Reading visually is a skill that should be taught in every discipline.

Figure 2.3

Cartoon Related to Science Content

"Perhaps one of you gentlemen would mind telling me just what it is outside the window that you find so attractive...?"

Source: Cartoon by Nick D Kim, scienceandink.com. Used with permission.

Extend and Adapt

Have students create their own visuals after reading, but be sure to give them plenty of models to guide their creations and provide time for students to google a variety of infographics. They should select examples that they think are especially effective and work in groups to analyze the graphic and explain why it works. Finally, ask them to create a graph based on your topic of study.

As an example, look at the "Whaling Is a Big Issue" infographic from the Humane Society of America. Then, try this:

- Ask students to take an overall look at the visual to determine its main idea.

- Then, ask how reading a chart or infographic differs from reading print-based text: Do they "read" left to right, top to bottom, or back and forth, for example?

- Next, ask students to connect the statements in the graph to the images. Why might the creator have used a particular image?

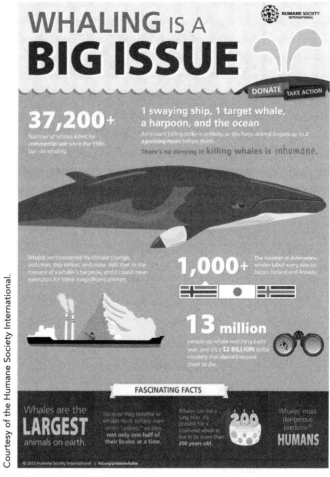

This whaling infographic from the Humane Society International provides an opportunity for students to practice visual literacy skills.

- Have students determine which feature or illustration the creator most wanted them to notice. Why might he or she have created the visual in that way?

- Allow students to express their own observations, which at times are insightful, such as when a student said he would have put the statement, "Whales' most dangerous predator? Humans." front and center because that seemed to him the whole point of the infographic.

After analyzing the infographic about whaling, eighth graders in a team-taught science and math class created their own infographics of animals that are in danger of extinction. They also developed guidelines to direct their work, focusing on how to make their communication clear to other readers. The questions they developed for the creation of their infographics follows.

1. What do we want readers to understand?

2. How will we find powerful images that show readers what we are trying to communicate?

3. Where will we find "fascinating facts"? How will we know the facts are accurate?

4. How will we use numbers to make our point?

5. How will we balance words, numbers, and images to convince or inform our readers?

4. ENTERING THE BLOGOSPHERE: TEXT FROM THE REAL WORLD

World Book Encyclopedias once offered articles on everything from artichokes to zebras, but in the 21st century, such articles are found not only on Wikipedia and related websites but also in blogs from experts in the field. Some are not so great (or so credible), but others, such as those from the *New York Times* or *Scientific American*, exhibit top-notch professional writing. As teachers in this technological era, we must show our students how to read, evaluate, and write in this venue.

Spotlight on ELA and Social Studies Team-Taught Class

Contributed by Tim Kramer, middle school social studies teacher

Tim Kramer and Michele Kandl

Mariam Fuzail, one of Tim and Michelle's students, created this picto-wordle.

Michele Kandl, an ELA teacher, and I team-teach a lesson we created for the introduction of a unit on Mesopotamia. We first grouped the kids by the stems of social studies we call *GRAPES*: geography, religion, achievements, politics, economics, and social systems. The kids were tasked with becoming experts in their strand of social studies as they dug deeply into some articles we provided from *Calliope Magazine*. They then had to find two other sources on their own. The discussions we heard while they read for specific information were riveting examples of exploration and collaborative learning. The students were highly engaged and excited to share the information they discovered from the source material. It was "normal nonfiction reading," but the students felt they were discovering and exploring rather than simply reading what the teacher had given them.

With their research, they had to create a visual (which we termed a *picto-wordle*) to represent their understanding of their assigned strand. They also wrote a "help wanted" ad for an expert in their assigned field. Their ads and picto-wordles allowed us to assess students' understanding of how each strand of social studies is related to Mesopotamia.

This was the students' first experience with the strands of social studies in ancient history and the activity helped them "own" their specific strand. The students became invested in their work, and the visual literacy aspect of the project allowed them to show their understanding in a creative and meaningful way. More impressive, though, was seeing the kids react so positively to their classmates' beautiful and thoughtful presentations.

How It Works

Show students a reputable blog site related to your discipline and explain that a blog's major function is to communicate with other Web users around the world for the purpose of informing, interacting with, or persuading a large number of people.

Karen Castelli, a high school psychology and sociology teacher, introduces the subject of sociology to her students each semester by showing them several sociology blogs, asking what they have in common, why she considers them reputable, and directing them to analyze the topics they cover. "A particular favorite blog site of mine," she says, "is *Sociological Images* because the entries always start with a good media image followed by comments on the sociological implications of the ads, images, and programs. It's a great way to combine sociology with media literacy." She then gives students class time to read and summarize three blog entries from the site. She allows students to use the tag cloud at the foot of the page to choose topics that may be of particular interest to them, such as *social movements, friendships, commodification, tourism, aging,* and so forth.

Karen helps her students assess the blog entries in preparation for writing their own blogs later in the course. Read about how Karen has her students write blogs in Chapter 3.

Why It Works

Blogs are texts that show the differences in disciplinary reading in a way that often intrigues students, even those who may say they don't like to read.

In addition, blog writers often develop a "voice" that makes reading more appealing or easier to understand. These differences help students understand how language works to communicate, inform, or persuade in various disciplines as well as how to develop their own voice in writing. When texts are used to show students examples of good disciplinary writing, they are called *mentor texts*. To make my point, take a look at a few lines from some popular blogs in Figure 2.4 that could be used in different classes. In Gowers' weblog

Blogs are texts that show the differences in disciplinary reading in a way that often intrigues students, even those who may say they don't like to read.

Ideas for Using Blogs in the Classroom

- Provide two blogs reflecting opposing sides of an issue and ask students to read each, listing the arguments the writer makes in support of his position. Create charts and compare the arguments, discussing why one blog may be more effective than another.

- Have students read and evaluate blogs in terms of credibility and impartiality. They can underline "loaded" words that seek to influence rather than inform or circle phrases that are questionable or misleading. Then, have students compare blogs from two different blog sites and determine which they would recommend to someone interested in the topic and why. Students soon learn how to articulate or write about their evaluations of blogs, noting subtleties in various blogs that support their conclusion.

- Use blogs to help students understand the author's message. Ask: *What is the author saying? What does the author mean? How do you know?*

- Have students choose one blog per week to include in their learning logs along with a response to the writer.

for math, for example, notice how the author writes about a "simple general argument that can be used to work out formulae," common language for most mathematicians. The social studies blog assumes a humorous voice but the author makes his point about a popular topic in history, Neandertals. The English blog uses more flowery language, the science blog quotes Albert Einstein, and so forth. These distinctions are important for students to understand when reading disciplinary texts. Consider how you might use the blogs in Figure 2.4 and others in your discipline to show students how to read and write in your field.

Extend and Adapt

Go the *New York Times* Learning Network (learning.blogs.nytimes.com), a great site for innovative teachers, and find a blog that can be used across

Figure 2.4

Mentor Texts:
Examples From Popular Blogsites

GOWERS'S WEBLOG (MATH)

https://gowers.wordpress.com/2014/11/04/sums-of-kth-powers/

"Sums of kth powers"
November 4, 2014

Recently I was giving a talk at a school in London and had cause to think about sums of kth powers, because I wanted to show people the difference between unenlightening proofs and enlightening ones. (My brief was to try to give them some idea of what proofs are and why they are worth bothering about.) On the train down, I realized that there is a very simple general argument that can be used to work out formulae for sums of kth powers.

SCIENTIFIC AMERICAN (SOCIAL STUDIES/HISTORY/SCIENCE)

http://blogs.scientificamerican.com/observations/neandertals-turned-eagle-talons-into-jewelry-130-000-years-ago

"Neandertals Turned Eagle Talons into Jewelry 130,000 Years Ago"
by Kate Wong on March 12, 2015

Neandertals are the Rodney Dangerfields of the human family—they don't get no respect. Despite mounting evidence that our prehistoric cousins hunted with great skill, made beautiful stone tools, showed compassion toward one another and buried their dead, among other advanced behaviors, the word *Neandertal* remains a widely used pejorative.

BOOK WHISPERER (ELA)

http://the-bookwhisperer.blogspot.com/2012/01/perilous.html

Perilous
January 3, 2012

Tamara Heiner constructs a fantastic read that touched every one of my emotions. Fear clawed my stomach, urgency twisted my nerves, anticipation grated my brain. Yes, humor packaged the thrill perfectly where needed.

(Continued)

(Continued)

With the action so tight, it was bittersweet when the story slowed a bit toward the second half of the book. I was a bit confused toward the end with the way certain things were presented, but it didn't diminish my enjoyment. It's certainly a satisfying read.

USA SCIENCE AND ENGINEERING FESTIVAL: THE BLOG (SCIENCE)

http://scienceblogs.com/usasciencefestival/2015/03/20/the-quest-for-truth-what-scientists-can-learn-by-observing-nature

"The Quest for Truth: What Scientists Can Learn by Observing Nature"
Guest blog by USA Science & Engineering Festival X-STEM speaker Louie Schwartzberg on March 20, 2015

Albert Einstein remarked, "Look deep into nature, and then you will understand everything better." He knew something that many scientists and engineers overlook in their quest for truth: nature holds the answers we're seeking . . . Truthfully, the facts were written long before humans arrived on this planet and we are simply catching up. What science brings to the table is a deeper understanding of why things happen, and how to ensure the right things continue to happen so both our species and planet thrive together.

BALLHYPED (SPORTS)

http://ballhyped.com/2015/03/21/cowboys-sign-greg-hardy-but-at-what-cost

"Cowboys Sign Greg Hardy; But at What Cost?"
by Kodyssportskorner on March 21, 2015

The Dallas Cowboys made another splash in free agency when they signed free agent, Greg Hardy. But this signing comes with a lot of trepidation from the Cowboys fan base.

ART RAVELS (ART)

linneawest.com/the-black-unconscious-odilon-redons-lithographs-of-st-anthony

"The Black Unconscious: Odilon Redon's Lithographs of St. Anthony"
by Linnea West on February 1, 2015

I think of dreamy, smudged pinks and blues when I think of the work of Odilon Redon, the 19th century French Symbolist artist. However, a recurring concern of the artist was the temptation of St. Anthony by the devil, as told in a popular contemporary book by Gustave Flaubert, which Redon rendered in lithograph three times over the course of his life.

disciplines. Work with another teacher in a different discipline who has the same students and have him or her read the identical blog in each class with teachers showing how experts in each field might analyze the text differently.

Repeated readings with different purposes are great ways of helping students tackle challenging text, and the Learning Network has everything in one place, ready for you to access. For example, today I went on the site and found these topics:

- Should a College Education Be Free?
- Microsoft HoloLens: A Sensational Vision of the PC's Future
- Jan. 22, 1973: *Roe v. Wade* and the Death of L.B.J.
- Do You Ever Write About Challenges You Face in Life?
- Unlocking Scrolls Preserved in Eruption of Vesuvius, Using X-Ray Beams

My favorite blog on this page is *"Lord of the Flies* and *A Fight Club for Flies."* The authors, Susan Chenelle and Audrey Fisch, first talk about the classic novel *Lord of the Flies* and then make a connection from the themes in the novel to a science article and video from the about how flies can be extremely aggressive, much like the young boys in William Golding's novel. Imagine a science and ELA teacher teaming together to use this article with students as a way to deepen thinking about how novelists use scientific concepts to create symbolism.

5. UNLOCKING CHALLENGING TEXT: A COLLABORATIVE TAKE

I couldn't leave this chapter without addressing possibly the hottest topic in reading: close reading of challenging text. I added the *collaborative take* because I believe collaboration can be an important and engaging complement to close reading practices.

How It Works

The text you select for close reading should be short but challenging, and it should be complex enough to engage students over multiple readings. The purpose of close reading is to focus on comprehension, making meaning through careful and thoughtful examination of the text.

One way to choose a text for close reading is to find an article that has been divided into sections. For example, an article in *Time* magazine for high school science students titled "New Ways to Disrupt Aging" (Park, 2015) is a long and complex text about how a drug used on mice may unlock the secret to aging. It is divided into four parts:

- Introduction—7 paragraphs
- A Modern Antiaging Elixir—8 paragraphs
- Find the Switches to Flip—7 paragraphs
- So Simple and So Strange—6 paragraphs

Similarly, an article in *Smithsonian* titled "Myths of the American Revolution" (Ferling, 2010) is divided into seven parts. Make sure you provide enough background information and conceptual vocabulary understandings to ease frustration, and it is often helpful to read the first paragraph aloud to everyone. Then, provide the first section to every student.

Instructions for Close Reading Activity

1. Ask students to read the first section quickly, just to get the gist.

2. Then, have students read the section again, more carefully this time, annotating as they go through the section by

   - Circling (or highlighting) any words or concepts with which they are unfamiliar
   - Underlining anything which they find confusing or which they question
   - Bracketing the best sentence (or phrase) in the text
   - Writing notes in the margin, on sticky notes or with the editing tool on their electronic device

3. Place (or allow students to gather) into groups of three to four to talk through their annotations. Make sure you are available to answer questions or clear up misconceptions.

4. Pass out the next section and repeat the procedure. You may wish to mix up the process to keep interest high, such as allowing students to read the section aloud in pairs or taking turns reading orally.

5. When the entire article has been read by everyone (which may take more than one class period), have students work together in their groups to answer questions similar to the following. Give students a time limit and have a student facilitator keep things moving so everyone has a chance to contribute.

Students in Karen Castelli's class read and respond to another group's contributions.

   - What questions or confusion still remains about the text?

   - What three points would you like to make to the author, perhaps in a letter to the editor?

   - If the author wrote a follow-up article, what would you like for him to address?

   - Which section did you find the most difficult to read? Why?

   - Write the author's best sentence.

6. Groups may post their answers on chart paper, tape the charts to the wall in various places, and move around the room reading the contributions of other groups. Or, you may prefer to have students present their responses to one or more of the questions to the whole class as a prompt for further discussion.

Why It Works

This activity slows down the process, relieves the pressure to comprehend immediately (or the urge to give up), and allows students to work collaboratively to find meaning. Besides increasing comprehension, students ask questions that they may not put forth in a whole-class discussion. It also allows the teacher to engage in formative assessment, noting which students need additional help.

Extend and Adapt

Scaffold the process by providing challenging text in very short segments (such as lists, word problems, or directions for a procedure). George Washington's *Rules of Civility* is an example of such a text because the rules are written in archaic language and refer to contexts and situations unfamiliar to students. Have students work together as they seek to understand the rules by engaging in the following activity.

Place students in triads and give each student a set of ten "rules."

- Student A will read the Rule #1,
- Student B will summarize Rule #1 (at first haltingly and with great humor) and then he will read Rule #2.
- Student C will summarize Rule #2 and then read Rule #3.

The process continues until all rules are read and students have taken turns attempting to summarize them.

Nicolas Yeager

This senior had never been interested in reading before entering Nicolas Yeager's senior English survey class. Nicolas says, "With the freedom, structured time, and trust that students are afforded in this class, many students read an equivalent of one novel (200–250 pages) a week in books of their own choosing—in addition to doing all of the work necessary for credit replacement."

Students then read the rules again, this time individually, placing a check beside the ones that are appropriate for today and a star beside the ones that seem ridiculous for today. When they come back together, they discuss their choices and then complete the following task to share with the class.

- Which one rule that you were given is still applicable today? Why?
- Which one rule that you were given is most ridiculous for today's society? Why?
- Create a new rule that is important for students to follow today.

I facilitated this activity with a group of eighth-grade "non-readers," and every single group was able to read the rules and do the activity. In the end, students engaged in reflection of their learning and expressed pride in their accomplishments, rating themselves as better readers than they had previously thought.

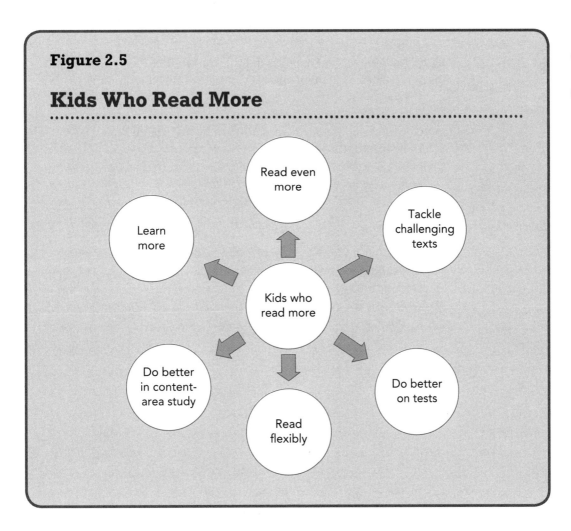

Figure 2.5

Kids Who Read More

As you can see, the theme of this chapter is that reading in the disciplines matters—a great deal. The cumulative effect will help students understand content and perform better in their future endeavors, whether that turns out to be college or career. There is simply no downside to reading frequently, widely, and voraciously.

Suggestions for Further Reading

Adolescent Literacy in the Academic Disciplines: General Principles and Practical Strategies by Tamara L. Jetton and Cynthia Shanahan (Eds.), 2012.

Classroom Instruction That Works: Research-Based Strategies for Increasing Student Achievement by Robert J. Marzano, Debra J. Pickering, and Jane E. Pollock, 2001.

Engaging Adolescents in Reading by John T. Guthrie, 2007.

"Factors Related to Amount and Type of Leisure Time Reading" by Vincent Greaney, 1980.

GuysRead Website: http://guysread.com/

How Students Learn: Science in the Classroom by M. Suzanne Donovan and John D. Bransford (Eds.), 2005.

Overcoming Textbook Fatigue: 21st Century Tools to Revitalize Teaching and Learning by ReLeah Cossett Lent, 2012.

Reading Like a Historian: Teaching Literacy in Middle and High School History Classrooms by Sam Wineburg, Daisy Martin, and Chauncey Monte-Sano, 2013.

Reading Unbound: Why Kids Need to Read What They Want—And Why We Should Let Them by Jeffrey Wilhelm and Michael W. Smith (with Sharon Fransen), 2014.

Text-Dependent Questions: Pathways to Close and Critical Reading, Grades 6–12 by Douglas Fisher and Nancy Frey, 2014.

Making it Relevant

1. Think about one unit you teach in your discipline. How could you begin creating a text set of articles, websites, visuals, fiction, and nonfiction for this unit? What might you want to include?

2. The elephant in the room is often this question: "How can I incorporate more reading and still cover my content?" With an increased understanding of the importance of reading in your content area, how would you answer that question?

3. In looking at the shifts needed to incorporate disciplinary literacy on page 15, what might you add to that list?

Notes:

3

WRITING *WITHIN* THE DISCIPLINES

Of the many eloquent and compelling definitions of what it means to write, the most insightful might have been expressed by Gloria Park many years ago, "Writing is a way of knowing."

An expanded analysis of writing comes in the College Board's report, *The Neglected R:* "If students are to make knowledge their own, they must struggle with the details, wrestle with the facts, and rework raw information and dimly understood concepts into language they can communicate to someone else. In short, if students are to learn, they must write" (2003, p. 9).

Students in Colleen Zenner's high school science class jot down notes to organize their thinking before beginning a project.

Unfortunately, writing is still often overlooked in many subjects, even in some English Language Arts (ELA) classes, as the drive to *cover* content supersedes the need to *understand* content through writing. When writing is incorporated, it is often used as assessment rather than as a process for deepening learning. Furthermore, teachers of content areas do not see themselves as writing teachers—and often not as writers.

When asked to get on board with the school's new writing initiative, for example, a high school science teacher expressed frustration that she was expected to have students write lab notes in complete sentences with proper punctuation. "I want students to accurately jot down what they observe and not flower up their reports with metaphors or spend valuable time trying to figure out if a word needs to be capitalized," she explained. A math teacher spoke up in agreement, noting that he would be fine with having students interpret a graph in writing but didn't want them to write a poem about algebraic equations. Finally, one teacher said what everyone was thinking: "We have our own content to teach and we hardly have enough time to cover that—now we're supposed to teach writing? Isn't that a part of the English curriculum?"

In the past, the answer to that question would have been an unequivocal "yes," but recent research challenges the assumption that writing should be taught primarily in ELA classes. The reason? Writing varies so much from one discipline to the next that it is hard to define *good writing* as we may have done in the past. In fact, Arthur Applebee and Judith Langer (2013) point out that "the skills and strategies that work well for writing in an English class may not lead to effective writing in other subjects" (p. 7). Writing, as well as reading, is now understood to be rooted *within* the content areas, not across them.

Benefits of Writing Within the Disciplines

While writing has been a mainstay in social studies and ELA classes for years, we are now discovering the immense benefits of writing in math and science. Judy Willis, neurologist and teacher, has been championing the value of writing for some time because of its positive effects on learning and, amazingly, the brain itself. She recently wrote

> when it comes to math and science, writing brings more than literacy and communication advantages. The practice of writing can enhance the brain's intake, processing, retaining, and retrieving of information. Through writing, students can increase their comfort with and success in understanding complex material, unfamiliar concepts, and subject-specific vocabulary. When writing is embedded throughout the curriculum, it promotes the brain's attentive focus to classwork and homework, boosts long-term memory, illuminates patterns, gives the brain time for reflection, and when well-guided, is a source of conceptual development and stimulus of the brain's highest cognition. (Willis, 2011; originally published 2011© Edutopia.org; George Lucas Educational Foundation)

According to Willis (2011), writing is one of the most valuable practices teachers can use to further deep learning and creativity while supporting academic, social, and emotional intelligence. If there is a learning elixir, it may well be writing.

If there is a learning elixir, it may well be writing.

Shifts for Teaching Writing Within the Disciplines

Just as we looked at shifts for teaching reading within the disciplines, there are concrete shifts teachers can make to support content through writing. Applebee and Langer's (2013) groundbreaking work on writing instruction in the disciplines provides four important challenges that relate specifically to the Common Core, next generation, and state standards—and many apply to the practice of writing:

- Maintaining a rich and broad curriculum
- Avoiding formulaic approaches to the teaching of writing
- Teaching argument well
- Embedding literacy in work appropriate to the discipline (p. 179)

I would include other, fairly easy changes teachers can make to take advantage of the magic of writing that are listed in the shaded box below.

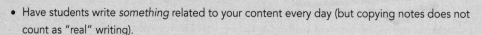

Shifts for Teaching Writing Within the Disciplines

- Have students write *something* related to your content every day (but copying notes does not count as "real" writing).
- Allow students to sometimes engage in written discourse with each other in place of discussing content: responses to each other's entries in learning logs or quick notes to each other regarding a complex problem, for example.
- Tell students early in the course that writing is learning and expect that all students will write.
- Use technology such as blogs and wikis to engage students in writing.
- Provide relevant tasks (such as real problems) and authentic audiences whenever possible to mirror real work in your discipline.
- Use writing as a type of formative assessment to guide instruction.
- Provide constructive feedback more often than corrective comments.
- Think of nonlinguistic representations such as drawings, symbols, or other visual text as writing when appropriate for your content.
- Don't worry about trying to be an English teacher (unless you *are* an English teacher). Teach writing as it relates to your discipline.

Teaching writing is similar to teaching reading: Each discipline has something different to offer students, and they need to experience writing from every academic angle. How does writing vary among the disciplines? Let's look at each one individually.

Writing Within Science

Traditionally, science writing has been limited to copying notes (or taking notes as a teacher lectures) and creating lab reports, which often are so formulaic that the writing is rote, requiring little thinking. Most often, as noted earlier, writing has been used as a method to test recall of information, not necessarily as a way of building knowledge or making sense of growing understandings. As one student said of her recent writing experience in ninth grade, "We copied notes from each other. We just needed to have something from each chapter in our notebooks."

In classes where writing is used as a tool for thinking and understanding, science teachers incorporate a variety of practices to motivate students to write reflectively and thoughtfully each day. Many use interactive notebooks or science journals where students do more than answer questions; they draw illustrations or charts, write about observations, or engage in written dialogues with another student "scientist." Such tools might include vocabulary charts where students conceptualize key terms through illustrations or connections, or they might even write stories about processes. One chemistry teacher redesigned the lab report so that students were better able to engage in thoughtful analysis by responding to the following questions:

- What do you see?
- And after data collection,
    o What do you think now?
    o What do you believe?
    o What does it mean?

The teacher extended the lesson by asking students to reflect through the question "Why do you care?" (Nachowitz, 2013, p. 107).

Characteristics of Writing Within Science

Scientific writing has the following characteristics:

- Technical, precise vocabulary is essential.
- Accuracy and exactness are favored over elaboration or craft.
- Verbs such as *demonstrate* are often changed to nouns such as *demonstration*.
- Observations are often written in bullet points, lists, or phrases.
- Sentence fragments or questions may be turned into complete thoughts only if the goal is to communicate.
- Passive voice is preferred, such as "The result was determined to be" in place of the active voice used in ELA classes, such as "I determined that . . ."
- Words may be minimal, used in conjunction with illustrations, charts, drawings, or data.
- Communication of ideas is clear and often systematic.
- Correctness is paramount but "overclaiming" is suspect.
- Descriptions of natural phenomena or the exploration of problems that have no definite solution may seem "wandering" or disorganized, especially when written as observations.

Students who learn to write in science must have many opportunities to engage with content, generate questions, reflect on new learning, and use writing as a tool for thinking.

Writing Within History and Social Studies

Social studies as a discipline has always valued writing as a way of interpreting, organizing, and clarifying the many dimensions of the subject. In fact, a position statement from the National Council of Social Studies (NCSS; 2008) states clearly that "Challenging social studies instruction makes use of regular writing." Students are expected to analyze and synthesize material across texts in writing, as evidenced by the document-based questions that dominate social studies curricula and tests.

Perhaps the most significant deterrent to writing within social studies is the push to cover so many topics, but, again, the NSSC encourages that key concepts and themes be developed in depth and that teachers "not diffuse their efforts by covering too many topics superficially" (2008). Such depth requires many forms of writing.

Forms of Writing Within History and Social Studies

The many creative and varied forms of writing that are available to social studies teachers may include the following:

- Response journals for current events, topics of study, or primary-based documents

- Timelines with accompanying narratives or illustrations

- Research on topics to expand and communicate new learning

- Summarization and synthesis of events from multiple sources

- Investigations of events and writing from a certain time period

- Biographical reports

- Interviews with experts in your field (see pages 132–134 for more information)

- Graphic organizers or essays that show comparison/contrast, cause/effect, major event/contributing factors, or sequence of events

- Argumentative essays defending a position based on evidence

- Short stories or other creative writing based upon historical events

- Writing for social justice causes

- News articles, song lyrics, speeches, or diaries created during a particular time period in history

There is no one way of writing in social studies because the topics and genres are so broad, as we see in the shaded box on page 19. Especially in this discipline, teachers can utilize writing every day in some form as students reinforce and internalize their understanding of history and social studies.

Writing Within Math

Math is a bit trickier when it comes to literacy because math "language" is composed of representations and symbols.

For that reason, there is very little writing in most math classrooms, though there is strong evidence that when students explain their thinking through writing in math classes, they deepen conceptual understandings (Mastroianni, 2013).

The most common writing application in math is the open-ended response question, which may resemble multiple-part word problems where students explain, justify, describe, estimate, or analyze mathematical calculations. They may also be asked to persuade others of their reasoning or adapt math to real-world situations where they create a plan or explain a construction. Often, a prewriting activity, such as the one in Figure 3.1, is useful so students can think through the process before beginning the writing. After prewriting, students may be ready to address a prompt similar to the following: Explain how you will solve the problem. Include reasons, supporting details, and examples when appropriate.

Tina Reckamp, middle school math teacher, created a website to help other teachers promote the use of literacy in math. She calls it "Read Math, Write Now." See Spotlight on Math on page 70 for her suggestions for helping teachers incorporate writing into math curricula.

Math is a bit trickier when it comes to literacy because math "language" is composed of representations and symbols.

Figure 3.1

Prewriting Prompts for a Math Problem or Concept

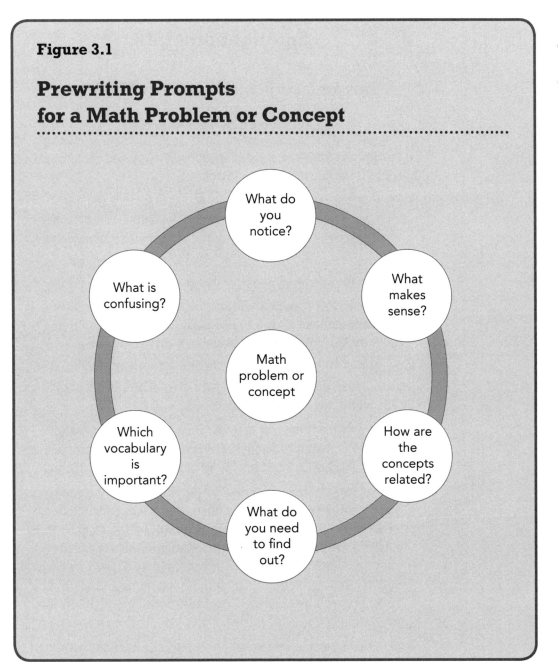

Spotlight on Math

Tips for Incorporating Literacy Into Math

Contributed by Tina Reckamp

- Provide a picture/visual that corresponds to the writing prompt or concept you are currently teaching.

- Try the "less is more" strategy: Students are given a small writing space such as a quarter sheet of paper. Have them fill up the entire small space which seems less intimidating than a whole sheet of paper.

- Use a math word wall to help with vocabulary.

- Treat math story problems just as you would a story. Identify characters and main ideas in the math story. This makes it much easier for kids to talk and write about math.

- Incorporate math pen pals/letter writing. Students share ideas about math with students in another math class or another content-area class within the same school.

- Be okay with writing just to write. Sometimes, students write about their goals for the quarter, reflections on their work, or even a "Dear Teacher" letter. Ongoing writing is essential in creating literacy in math.

- Let students respond to one another. After having them write for several minutes about a prompt, ask students to swap writing notebooks with a classmate and respond in some way, such as adding an additional idea to their peer's notebook, writing about whether they agree with their partner's reasoning and so on. The students now have an audience for their writing, which provides motivation.

- Utilize two-column writing when appropriate. Options with this are limitless. Students divide their paper into two columns with a vertical line. On one side, they might record main ideas of the section and on the other questions about the ideas—or key math words on one side and a rating of their understanding of the words on the other.

- Provide problems along with their answers and have students justify why the answer is correct or incorrect.

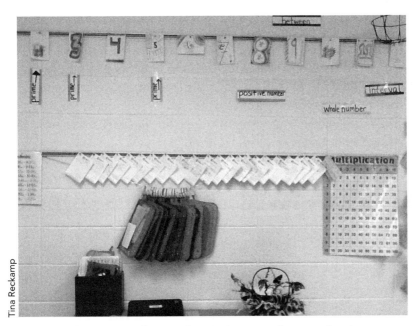

Tina created an activity where students write on small note pads using new vocabulary words. Classmates respond with "I agree" or "I disagree" and state why. They then pass their pads back to the original writer. Tina hangs the pads on the wall for all of her students to see.

Writing Within ELA

It may seem redundant to address writing in ELA since writing seems synonymous with the discipline itself, but a national survey conducted by Applebee and Langer (2013) found that while students may write more in ELA classes than in other disciplines, the writing often does not emphasize problem solving and inquiry or engage students in

extended writing projects. You can guess the type of instruction commonly found in many ELA classes: writing in preparation for high-stakes testing. Unfortunately, this approach not only limits students' range of writing opportunities but creates formulaic approaches that are counterproductive to learning through writing.

Teaching students how to write well by focusing on context, purpose, and audience prepares them for the demands of a timed essay in ways that stilted practice simply cannot.

Many ELA teachers contend that they are the only ones left to address the test-taking genre, and that may be true, but a focus on disciplinary writing across all content areas will better prepare students for standardized tests than isolated test prep in ELA classes. And there really is little evidence to show that such instruction improves test scores. In fact, teaching students how to write well by focusing on context, purpose, and audience prepares them for the demands of a timed essay in ways that stilted practice simply cannot.

Exemplary Practices for Writing in ELA

Exemplary practices for writing in ELA include the following:

- Engaging in the workshop approach where the process of writing is integrated in all writing instruction

- Providing solid mentor texts and analyzing good writing to show students some of the moves that effective writers make; asking students to try imitating these moves

- Teaching students how to provide effective peer feedback (see Figure 3.2)

- Allowing time for students to respond to one another's writing and for revision of their own work

- Organizing study and writing around big ideas and essential questions

- Engaging students in a wide variety of writing genres and tasks

- Focusing on content overcorrectness

- Explicitly teaching students how to generate ideas, organize thoughts, and write with clarity

- Avoiding formulaic writing—and that includes the five-paragraph essay, which is a contrived construct for most "real" writing

- Encouraging writers through positive, targeted, and timely feedback

Spotlight on ELA (With a Beam of Math)

Imagine students writing for disciplinary purposes in every subject, every day, immersed, as most standards envision, in a wide variety of writing in all sorts of genres. In fact, it's hard to believe that students could possibly meet the CCSS and other standards' goals of developing compelling and complex pieces of writing that inform and persuade when they have little experience "wallowing" in words, experimenting with how different phrases create different effects, or feeling the satisfaction in having created a piece of writing that hits its mark. Students must try on the many types of writing required in each discipline in order to become fluent and confident writers capable of manipulating language to serve their purposes.

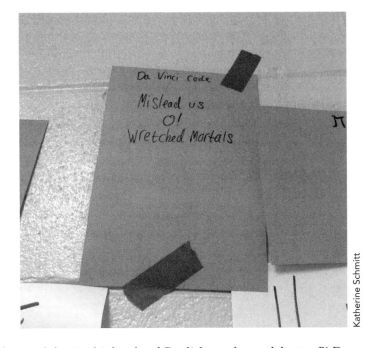

Katherine Schmitt, high school English teacher, celebrates Pi Day (March 14) by having her students write piku instead of haiku. She says, "Whereas a haiku is written in 5-7-5, a piku is written in 3-1-4. I asked them to write a piku of a book they have read." She then hangs all of the pikus on her classroom wall.

Questions (and Answers) About Writing Within the Disciplines

One of the reasons that I don't assign more writing is that I simply don't have time to grade 150 essays a week on top of the work students produce for my content. Any advice?

Where did we get the idea that every word students write has to be assessed, assigned a grade, and duly recorded to create a score that somehow reflects the writing worth of a student? Writing, as the National Council of Teachers of English (NCTE) (2008) maintains, "is not created by a singular, linear process; it cannot be taught, like bike riding, as a single skill; it changes with shifting technologies . . . it takes many forms; and it cannot be assessed effectively in a single sitting" (p. 3).

NCTE further argues that writing assessment is most effective during the context of instruction (in other words, when students are writing) and by utilizing a "carefully organized system of classroom documentation of student learning, through portfolios or other methods of collecting student work samples" (p. 6). Allow students to choose from among their many writing samples the one or two they want to turn into a full essay—and give them plenty of time to revise with lots of ongoing feedback from you and their peers. (See the next question regarding feedback.)

And while you're at it, consider a holistic grade on some compositions. Once again, NCTE (2008) comes to our rescue and helps us understand why all of our time *should not* be spent meticulously correcting students' writing: "Current research suggests that a holistic approach to instruction and assessment will give students the tools they need to develop as writers. A holistic approach sees writing as a multidirectional and multifaceted activity and attempts to teach and assess the many disparate aspects of writing in a connected fashion" (p. 4–5).

The most important thing I can say in answer to this question is that students should have many, many opportunities to write—with reduced pressure on the teacher to formally assess each piece of writing. Since writing is a process that develops over time and in response to different disciplinary purposes, back away from grading writing, especially daily writing, as much as possible and focus on engaging students in the process. Think in terms of rewarding effort and encouraging students

Students must try on the many types of writing required in each discipline in order to become fluent and confident writers capable of manipulating language to serve their purposes.

to take the intellectual risks needed to think deeply through writing. Remember, they are writing to learn.

I know that I should offer feedback when students write, but I'm not really sure how to do that. How does feedback differ from comments I make when I grade students' papers?

First, feedback is usually given during the process of writing so that it can be used by students to improve their writing before producing any kind of final draft. Such timely feedback functions as a type of formative assessment (used to monitor student learning), which helps teachers understand where students might need help and then provide additional instruction. In contrast, grades on completed papers are a form of summative assessment (used to evaluate learning) and are given after the fact. Corrective comments that students see for the first time when their papers are returned to them is like someone helpfully recommending a good mechanic after you've spent thousands of dollars having your car repaired—and it's still sputtering. You need advice when you're engaged in writing, not when it is too late.

I like to think of feedback as comments you would make to an adult in the field who asked your advice on a piece of writing.

- Is the piece clear?
- What more is needed?
- What works well?
- Has the writer accomplished his purpose?

Try to avoid telling the student what to do; instead, ask questions, explain why you are confused, amazed, or want more details and let her do the work of revising the piece based on your comments and the comments of peers, who should also be providing feedback.

See Figure 3.2 for examples of feedback that may be helpful as students rework their writing.

Should I always use a rubric?

In real-world writing, we write for a purpose, not for a rubric; and those purposes will vary widely, such as writing for understanding, analysis, persuasion, reflection, narration, or simply to communicate. Sometimes, a rubric narrows students' writing and thinking by artificially focusing the student on isolated components of writing. There is a place for rubrics, for example when students are writing an explanation of a process and they need to include specific steps for the process to be correct and complete. We also want to make sure students know what is expected and that they address the learning target. At other times, however, especially when writing is being used to reflect, learn, or understand, a rubric may not be appropriate, as the purpose involves exploration rather than a perfect end product.

It's better to think in terms of what the piece of writing needs to convey in order to be effective rather than always matching it to a rubric. If you do use a rubric, talk students though each part of the rubric and allow them to have a voice in what should be included in the tool. The process of having students decide what is important in a specific piece of writing sometimes turns out to be more valuable than the rubric itself.

Spotlight on Science

Colleen Zenner and Lauren Pennock, high school science teachers, have their students create a story about plate tectonics and follow a checklist that guides their work.

First, they provide directions:

- Write a story about plate tectonics that is creative, accurate, and helps explain to someone how the Earth is always changing.

- Include all of the items from the checklists (sample below) on each page of your story.

- Use your review sheets, unit packet, flashcards, and any other resources to help you explain the concepts.

- Create at least three characters that will journey through your story of plate tectonics.

Following are samples of some of the checklists and questions (with associated values) that students must address within the story to gain a total of 140 points:

- Characters with descriptions and illustrations (9 points)

- Introduction of character (3 points)

- Introduction of storyline (3 points)

- Conclusion to the storyline (3 points)

- What are four pieces of evidence for continental drift (explained)? (8 points)

- What are two types of plates? (2 points)

- What mechanism causes plates to move? (2 points)

- Did you include a definition of the *asthenosphere*? (2 points)

Won't the teaching of writing take time away from my content?

As you can see from the Spotlight on Science (page 77), writing is an often overlooked tool for reinforcing, expanding, and supporting content. There are many ways of incorporating writing within any lesson—a quickjot, for example, in a learning log in response to a thoughtful question or a silent discussion, where students write to each other about a problem. If you think writing means assigning a major essay every week, then it *will* take away from the content, especially in math or science. But writing to learn, writing to integrate ideas or figure out *why*, or writing to reinforce a new concept—that *is* content.

Writing to learn, writing to integrate ideas or figure out why, or writing to reinforce a new concept—that IS content.

Think of writing as a sort of glue that makes thoughts stick; research shows that's exactly what it is if it's used regularly (Willis, 2011).

Okay, here's the bottom line for me. I never took a writing course in college. What if I just don't know how to teach writing?

The good news is that you don't need to be a teacher of writing. You only need to show your students how scientists, mathematicians, historians, poets, musicians, or sports writers—whoever writes in your discipline—communicate through writing. Give them lots of examples from disciplinary-related texts such as journal articles, research, and blogs, and then illustrate how experts in your field use writing to expand the content you are teaching. Look at pages 51–52, Figure 2.4, to show students how bloggers write in your discipline, for example.

And here's the best part: You can learn to become a better writer along with your students as, together, you explore the best writing in your field. If you still feel unsure, ask an ELA teacher to give you some tips and start slowly. The great thing about disciplinary literacy is that you aren't expected to become a writer or a writing teacher—just a content-area teacher who lets kids in on the secrets of how people in your discipline write while giving them the opportunity to do the same.

Spotlight on Math

Amanda Cavicchioni, an eighth-grade algebra teacher, came up with an inventive way for students to apply their knowledge of quadratic equations by asking them to teach others about the concept. "Quadratic functions is a large unit in algebra, so I developed a project for my students to review and sum up what they learned by creating a how-to book," she says. "Each student picked a specific equation and demonstrated how to solve that equation using all five methods. I thought this would be a good way to help them make connections between the different ways of solving a quadratic functions as well as making connections between quadratic functions and other kinds of functions."

Students also had to write about which method they preferred to use when solving and had to include a page of real vocabulary and real-world examples. When they shared their products, the students were excited about how creativity could be used in math, evidenced by the clever themes and colorful drawings that made their stories come to life. Some said afterward that the books would be a useful study tool for the test they took after the project.

A student in Amanda Cavicchioni's class shows off her book on quadratic functions.

Shanna Dixon, high school algebra teacher, brings in real-world examples when she teaches parabolas. "After students learn about parabolas, I ask them to find and bring in examples of the curve in everyday life. Inevitably, someone brings in a photo of the St. Louis Arch and I have them write about why it may look like a parabola but really isn't one at all."

It's been a while since I've had an English course. Do I need to correct spelling or grammatical mistakes? I'm always worried that I'll miss something.

A social studies teacher said to me recently, "How can I get my students to write? They don't even know how to capitalize proper nouns." Real writing has little to do with grammar and rules—that's just the window dressing, which, increasingly, Word programs are able to address. I know an award-winning author who never really learned the "rules" of writing—but, man, can he write. The descriptive narratives, targeted metaphors, and compelling dialogue he composes bring tears to the eyes of the most hardcore technical writer.

Of course you should expect students to use the conventions of Standard English when they prepare a final draft of a formal paper, but you don't need to turn yourself into a grammar slave—or quash your students' desire to write by demanding grammatical perfection (or any other type of perfection) in the short writing they do in class. NCTE (2008) reassures us on this point when they state, "Surface-level feedback focused on grammar and spelling does not encourage students to develop their writing or thinking" (p. 4). They go on to say, "An exclusive focus on grammar instruction and grammar-related assessments can distract students and teachers from the entire range of features that constitute effective writing" (p. 5).

Here's a hint: When students write for a real audience, they are much more likely to pay attention to the mechanics of writing because they care. The real stuff of writing is being able to unravel a complex idea, express an idea of one's own, or use others' ideas, not create a grammatically correct piece that may be devoid of deep meaning.

The real stuff of writing is being able to unravel a complex idea, express an idea of one's own, or use others' ideas.

How to Get Students Writing Within the Disciplines

1. DIFFERENTIATED LEARNING LOG

Learning logs are not the content-area notebooks so ubiquitous in the 20th century. This writing tool, which can be created either

electronically or through print, is differentiated for each learner—
and is an essential tool in developing both content knowledge and
independence.

How It Works

Each student's learning log is kept with her at all times during class.
The log is not necessarily used to record new information because, as
we know, information is available to anyone at any time with the tap of
a finger. The purpose of this log is to hold ongoing reflection, analysis,
evaluation, and application of new information.

Many teachers like to have students use their logs during collaborative
activities such as when they participate in seminars or engage in
small-group work. It is important to note that the log belongs to the
student so no two will look exactly alike. Therefore, allow students
autonomy regarding its organization, decoration, and, to some extent, its
contents. If the teacher takes control of the "notebook," the motivation
for learning diminishes.

Why It Works

Differentiated instruction (DI) is one of those phrases that everyone
in education knows and most teachers strive to implement, but it
frequently falls between the cracks in the mad dash to cover content.
A differentiated learning log supports DI because it starts where all
individualized instruction must start: with the learner. Furthermore, each
student must take ownership of his own learning—and his own log—
which will serve different purposes as students learn how to organize the
many variables of content in ways that work for them.

Best of all, if teachers use learning logs in each discipline to show
students how discipline-area writing differs, students will increase their
understanding of writing overall.

Extend and Adapt

For students who have difficulty with organization, provide more
structure while still leaving room for autonomy. For example, you
may need to provide sample tables of contents or tell them how many
"found" vocabulary words you expect on their vocabulary page by the

Figure 3.3

What Goes Into a Learning Log?

- Observations gleaned from experiments, demonstrations, primary documents, or poetry
- Formative assessment pieces such as exit, entrance, or middle-of-class quickjots (see pages 91–92)
- Questions students may have during class, while doing homework, or during reading
- Summaries of and responses to texts, experiments, videos, music, or art
- Drawings, graphs, storyboards, graphic organizers, tables
- Rough drafts of writings: essays, fiction, articles, blogs, tweets
- Rules to remember: for example, punctuation rules, order of operation, scientific processes
- Clippings or copies of article, blogs, photographs; website links
- Quotes from texts, experts, or other students
- Project ideas (especially useful for social studies and science fairs as well as interdisciplinary or independent projects)
- Narratives, journals entries
- Song lyrics related to topics
- Primary documents and analyses
- Collaborative notes from group work or projects
- Books to read
- Writing ideas
- Vocabulary pages where students records words that are new to them or used in different ways. Note: If teachers want students to record vocabulary they have assigned, this should be in a different section or on a separate page.
- T-charts for learning:
  o Confusion/Get it
  o Really?/But
  o Agree/Disagree
  o Word Used/Better Word

end of a grading period. Have students share ways of organizing learning with each other instead of insisting on only one way.

2. BELL-RINGER QUESTIONS AND ANSWERS

Bell-ringer questions prime students' brains for academic tasks, often jolting their minds away from the conversation they had in the hall before class or their intriguing plans for lunch. This type of informal writing is probably also the best type of practice for "writing for the test," as it eases writer's block and counterproductive overthinking.

How It Works

Before class, place a question on the screen—not a typical textbook question, but a question that builds background about your content and the world students inhabit, a question that requires thinking, evaluating, and making decisions, which, by the way, also encourages independence (see Figure 3.4 for examples). Students write in their learning log (either electronically or on paper) in response to the query. For this activity, students simply pen a flood of words in an effort to craft some sort of answer to a less-than-simple question. Books such as *Super Freakonomics* (Levitt & Dubner, 2009), *What If?: Serious Scientific Answers to Absurd Hypothetical Questions* (Munroe, 2014) or websites featuring the latest news in science (National Science Foundation, www.nsf.gov/discoveries), social studies (the history website at www.history.com/news/ask-history), math (the math section of Scientific American at www.scientificamerican.com/math), or Smithsonian's Tween Tribune (tweentribune.com) are great sources for questions. After discussing and modeling how to craft good questions, students can begin submitting bell-ringer questions for their classmates to address in writing.

Why It Works

An often overlooked but important part of writing is fluency, the ability to write without anxiety or fear, allowing words to flow unimpeded on the page or screen.

Fluency develops when students are provided with frequent opportunities to jot down their thinking with no assessment attached.

Figure 3.4

Sample Questions for Bell-Ringer Writing

- The Curiosity's journey to Mars cost eight billion dollars. Was that money well spent? Why or why not?

- What should the United States do to make sure contagious diseases don't spread to major cities?

- What young adult novel would you recommend be made into a movie? Why?

- Why is immigration such a complex issue?

- Explain this statistic: Ratio of seriously mentally ill people held in US state prisons and jails to those held in state psychiatric hospitals: 10:1. (harpers.org/archive/2014/06/harpers-index-362) What should be done about this problem?

- What conflict do many characters share in novels or short stories? Is it a realistic conflict based on your own experiences?

- Why do people engage in forms of rioting that bring about more harm than good to their causes?

- Cemetery space is becoming a premium in many areas, especially large cities. Should cities pass laws that allow only cremation?

Many inexperienced writers fall into the trap of sitting for long periods of time before beginning to write as they compose in their heads. They then try to capture their ideas on paper, turning writing into a mechanical process of recording thoughts instead of utilizing writing as a tool for thinking. The daily practice of writing in response to open-ended questions supports fluency and gives students ideas for future essays in addition to helping them think deeply about content-area topics.

Extend and Adapt

Follow writing sessions with a reading connection in the form of a brief read-aloud from a text related to the question, giving students just enough to make them want to find out more on their own. Provide a link to the article or make available copies of the printed article for those who want to read about the topic. For instance, post this question in a science class that has been studying alternative fuel sources: A bus in the UK went into service that runs on an unusual type of fuel. What type of fuel do you think the bus is using? Defend your answer.

The fuel? Human waste from a sewage plant. After students express their disgust, provide the article for their reading pleasure.

3. READ/THINK/RESPOND

A response differs from an analysis in that writers interpret the text through a subjective stance, making connections and bringing background knowledge as they seek to interpret the author's message. The goal is to eventually move students into analysis, but often a response is the first and best way of getting to that point. As the term implies, students react to what they are reading in any way they can, often beginning such writing with "I think" or "It seems like" in an attempt to understand the text. In some cases, the text may be so complex that students don't know how to respond, but with this low-risk activity they feel they can say *something*, opening the path for more in-depth writing later.

Math students in particular often find "a place to start" by wrestling with a problem through a response. In fact, research shows that some writing activities have a greater impact on reading comprehension than reading strategies (Lewis, Walpole, & McKenna, 2014). This may well be one of those activities.

An often overlooked but important part of writing is fluency, the ability to write without anxiety or fear, allowing words to flow unimpeded on the page or screen.

How It Works

This activity is easy and effective.

1. Students read a short piece of complex text related to your discipline.
2. They think for a few moments about the text.
3. They write a response to the text.

As an example, let's take a letter from Queen Victoria to Mary Todd Lincoln after the death of President Lincoln, found in the Library of Congress at memory.loc.gov/cgi-bin/query/r?ammem/mal:@ field(DOCID+@lit(d4363400))

Figure 3.5

Queen Victoria to Mary Todd Lincoln, Saturday, April 29, 1865 (Condolences)

From Queen Victoria to Mary Todd Lincoln,[1] April 29, 1865
Osborne.
April 29—1865.

Dear Madam,

Though a stranger to you I cannot remain silent when so terrible a calamity has fallen upon you and your country, and most personally express my deep and heartfelt sympathy with you under the shocking circumstances of your present dreadful misfortunes.

<u>No</u> one can better appreciate than <u>I</u> can, who am myself <u>utterly broken hearted</u> by the loss of my own beloved husband,[2] who was the light of my life,—my stay—my all,—what your sufferings must be; and I earnestly pray that you may be supported by Him to whom alone the sorely stricken can look for comfort in this hour of heavy affliction.

With the renewed expression of true sympathy,

I remain,

dear Madam,

your sincere friend,

Victoria

[Note 1 Victoria occupied the British throne from 1837 to 1901.]

[Note 2 Prince Albert, Victoria's husband of twenty-one years, died in 1861.]

Source: Courtesy of Library of Congress.

An eighth grader who often found it extremely difficult to even begin a piece of writing was told to simply read the text and write his thoughts. He wrote: "It seems like Queen Victoria was thinking more about herself than about Mrs. Lincoln." While this response is hardly a comprehensive analysis, it is a good time for the teacher to ask the student to explain his thinking. The student then wrote, "Well, the queen talked about her *heavy affliction* and how *broken-hearted* she was instead of asking Mrs. Lincoln how her heart was holding up." This student not only went back to the text, but he began moving toward a critical evaluation of the text.

This activity is especially effective for use with complex sections of the textbook, challenging poetry, or graphics that may be confusing.

Why It Works

Many times students shut down when faced with text that seems overly complex or challenging. Responding to the ideas in a text can be a nonthreatening way to help such students read actively and think about what the author is saying. While it may seem that this activity is time consuming, it is time well spent as students come to understand key components of a topic before rushing on to the next question, a practice that often compounds frustration and increases confusion.

Extend and Adapt

For students who have difficulty getting started, have them use a prewriting chart to keep their responses tied to the text instead of wandering off into tangential areas. A template might look something like the one in Figure 3.6.

4. TALK BACK

With this activity, students can enjoy doing what they do best: talking back. They can also learn the basics of argumentative writing, especially once they are writing responses fluently.

How It Works

Provide students with a provocative text, such as a blog from the *New York Times* about why medicinal marijuana should be legalized or a

Figure 3.6

Chart for Helping Students Formulate a Response

What did the author say? What was his/her message?	What in the text do you find insightful, interesting, confusing, or just plain wrong?	What do you think about the author's overall message? Why?

Huffington Post piece about children crossing the border from Mexico on top of a train, or even a new finding in science or math such as how artificial intelligence can now create magic tricks and what that might mean for the future. Have students read the text once to determine the author's stance. Then, ask them to read it again and choose a particular paragraph, sentence, claim, or idea brought forth by the author that they might question or want to think about further. In this talk-back activity, they write as if they were a colleague of the author's, asking questions, pointing out areas the author may not have thought through, or simply disagreeing with the author's accuracy or reasoning.

This procedure can also be used when students read an op-ed piece or commentary. They read (or listen to) the commentary, determine the author's point of view by noting what he says (and what he means) and then talk back by methodically refuting or agreeing with his points

The activity works best when there is some question about the topic or when the author is taking a strong, perhaps biased position. Paragraphs or sections from textbooks could be used, but opinion pieces, even from local newspapers, or letters to the editor are better suited for talking back. When a hot topic is hitting the news, YouTube videos or an online news snippet may work especially well. In any case, look for topics that represent controversial or thought-provoking issues in your discipline.

Example of a Hot-Button Talk Back

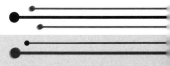

As I am writing this chapter, the trial of the Boston Bomber Dzhokhar Tsarnaev is under way. The defense maintains that he was under the influence of his brother, Tamerlan, but the prosecution is making the case that he was acting alone. Most students have siblings; many have very close brothers. They might talk back to either the defense or the prosecution about their viewpoint on this issue—after having read a text to gain background information such as the article from the *New York Times* at www.nytimes.com/2015/03/17/us/police-recall-dodging-as-marathon-bombing-suspect-ran-over-brother.html?ref=us. While this topic may elicit strong emotions, it creates an opportunity for students to learn how to express "hot" opinions in a calm, logical manner.

Example of a Talk Back in Questioning the Author

Questions help facilitate a process where students tease out their incredulity by providing reasons for their thinking, the basis of all good argumentative writing.

Recently, I read a chapter to a class of eleventh graders from the book *How They Croaked: The Awful Ends of the Awfully Famous* (Bragg, 2011) regarding Napoleon's pretty horrible death to demonstrate how voice can be used in a humorous way to inform. Immediately after the reading, a student told me that hundreds of books about Napoleon have been written (a quick Google search shows that he was exactly right) and that many authors had various hypotheses about the exact manner of Napoleon's death. "How does this author know these details about his death?" he asked. This student was, in effect, talking back to or questioning the author. It would have been an easy transition to move the class into writing by asking them to take out their learning logs and write about whether they agree or disagree with the veracity of the author's claims before looking up this information online from a credible source.

Similarly, a high school ELA student asked if Alice Walker was a credible source for her 2007 picture book titled *Why War Is Never a Good Idea*. While the book is more an example of stunning poetry than commentary, I encouraged the student to express his doubts and then asked the class to write their response to the author's ideas. Such questions help facilitate a process where students tease out their incredulity by providing reasons for their thinking, the basis of all good argumentative writing.

Why It Works

Argumentative writing starts first with argumentative thinking, and argumentative thinking begins with questioning instead of passively accepting what is read. (See Chapter 4 on Inquiry.) Embedding arguments within the topics of a discipline helps students see that argument (as well as agreement) comes organically from the study of an issue or, as Applebee and Langer (2013) note in *Writing Instruction That Works*, "Arguments and explanations within a discipline are built up out of the context of ongoing . . . conceptual learning" (p. 161).

Extend and Adapt

Once students have composed their talk-back piece, have them exchange and write back to each other, continuing the conversation or expanding argument. Eventually, this activity could be played out in a debate or forum, but only after students have had a chance to codify their thinking through writing. Students may also want to illustrate their essays with political cartoons or conduct interviews with those who have opposing perspectives.

To make easy work of this activity, check out the *New York Times* Learning Network (learning.blogs.nytimes.com) where well-written blogs appear along with questions for student writing and excellent teacher resource materials (see Chapter 2, pages 50 and 53). As a bonus, the site also offers a "word of the day" from the text. Debate.org also offers thought-provoking questions, often with student responses included.

5. EXIT, ENTER, MIDDLE-OF-CLASS QUICKJOT

The exit slip has become a popular activity in many classes, but I don't see it used often enough to bring about the advantages it can accrue. Some teachers say that the novelty of an exit slip wears off and students begin writing less thoughtfully, which is why I encourage variations of this practice, such as an entrance, middle-of-class, or just-about-anytime quickjot.

How It Works

Provide students with a list of prompts such as those in Figure 3.7 and post them on the wall for easy access. Ask students to add to the list. At regular intervals during class, have students compose quickjots on index cards or sticky notes to hand in to you. They may also write in their learning logs or on a device that can be checked by you periodically.

Why It Works

These quickjots can be invaluable in assessing student understanding of content, taking a quick pulse of the class's knowledge, or giving students a chance to codify what they are learning. In addition, when students write often to such prompts, they learn to use metacognitive skills in deciding for themselves how and what they are learning.

This activity shifts the ownership and responsibility for learning back to the students and teaches them to monitor their own understanding for intrinsic purposes, not simply to pass a test.

Quickjots can assess student understanding, provide a pulse of the class's knowledge, or give students a chance to codify what they are learning.

Figure 3.7

Prompts for Quickjots

- What do you "get" so far?
- What do you find confusing?
- How would you report on what you just learned for an online news article or blog?
- What did the author, problem, or lesson leave out that you would have included?
- What else do you want to know?
- What one piece of the problem, lab, poem, document, or short story is most important?
- How does the piece, poem, story, or blog affect you emotionally?
- What would you tweet to highlight today's lesson?
- Do you disagree with anything you read or something someone said in class about the text or lesson? Explain.

Extend and Adapt

Use students' quickjots as springboards for longer writing pieces by asking them to elaborate on their comments when appropriate. Once students compose more in-depth pieces, they can exchange with a partner and write questions about the explanation as a way of encouraging more detail and clarification from the original writer.

6. FROM CONTENT TO STORY

Use the power of narration to help students learn content-area concepts by having them create a story around an academic topic. Such writing, called by Tom Newkirk (2014) the "mother of all modes," is "a powerful and innate form of understanding." He further argues that narration can be used "to inform, to persuade, to entertain, to express" (p. 6), and I would add that it also creates a context for learning, engages students in writing, and reinforces important ideas in all disciplines.

How It Works

Think of topics in your content as stories; virtually all disciplines have them: weather cycles in science, sequential events in history, word problems in math, or biographies in the arts. Tracy Kalas, a middle school ELA teacher who works closely with math teachers in her grade level, came up with the idea of using mathematical vocabulary in stories that she has created, such as this one, titled "The Revolution of Literacy":

Students in Tina Reckamp's math class write simple exit slips to help Tina keep track of their progress. She posts their sticky-note exit slips under her learning objectives at the entryway to her class.

> Under the triangular roof of our angular school is an oval office where a set of ordered pairs pound out solutions to our problems. They are coefficients converging over discrete negative matters of orders of operation. Don't underestimate that this is where the chain of command rules.
>
> Clockwise, with the maximum function of power, is the principal who is not mean but midpoint between rational expression and irrational expression. At his right hand sits a fraction of his power . . .

Students love these stories and now are trying their hands at writing very creative short stories . . . in math class.

Examples of Narrative Within the Disciplines

Following are examples of ways that content-area teachers have engaged students in narrative writing to expand content understandings and perspectives:

- Write a journal entry from one of the Little Rock Nine about his or her preparations for going to school that first day in 1957.

- Write about the journey lava takes from its inception at the earth's molten core to its eruption and eventual solidification into rock.

- Write a story about the interpretation of the Second Amendment in the year 2050.

- Choose one example of an ancient architectural creation where the engineers used the Golden Ratio within its design. Write from the perspective of the designer about how the Golden Ratio helped him create one of the world's great wonders. Provide some intrigue in the story if possible!

- Write an interview with a survivor of the Triangle Shirtwaist Fire.

- Write about the "story" behind how someone influential came to change our thinking in science, social studies, math, or poetry.

Why It Works

Children in virtually every society begin their literate lives surrounded by stories, and stories continue to influence their lives, from movies to video games to historical accounts to conversations with friends. This genre engages because it transforms dry facts into fascinating details that stick long after the lesson has ended. Take advantage of this powerful form of writing to deepen content and provide an accessible way for students to become engaged in writing.

Extend and Adapt

If you have never used a strategy called RAFT (Role, Audience, Format and Topic) or it has been a while since you have utilized it in your discipline, dust it off and adapt it for your next unit. RAFT exercises lend themselves to narratives and help students understand content by approaching it in a new and creative way. See Figure 3.8 on page 96 for examples of RAFT prompts in various disciplines.

Spotlight on Science

After reading *Little Changes* by Tiffany Taylor to his group of freshman biology students, Justin Stroh had them create their own children's books about evolution and natural selection to be read to upper elementary students. His instructions included the following:

1. Create a population of organisms that is not real.

2. Describe a trait this population has and the variations of this trait in the population.

3. Discuss and illustrate the original environment of the population.

4. Create a change in the environment that will result in the population evolving over time.

5. Make sure the story demonstrates one of the three types of natural selection.

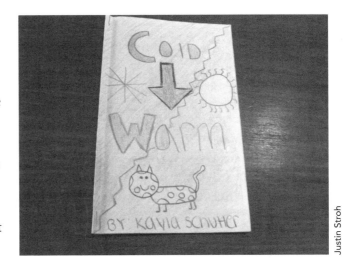

Cold/Warm booklet created by one of Justin's students about how a creature evolved to survive in a warmer climate.

Justin was pleased with the understanding of evolution that his students demonstrated through this engaging project.

7. BLOGGING IT UP

In Chapter 2, Karen Castelli, a high school sociology teacher, discusses how she uses blogs to initially interest students in her discipline through authentic reading. Karen also uses the blog format to have her students participate in writing, and she reports that their interest in writing has

Figure 3.8

Examples of RAFT Prompts in Various Disciplines

Discipline	Role	Audience	Format	Topic
ELA	Young Japanese boy living in the US during WWII	Undocumented immigrant detained in holding center	Letter	What have we done wrong?
Social Studies	Harry Truman	American people	News broadcast	Why I dropped the bomb
Science	Pancreas	Teenager	Tweet	Don't eat that Twinkie!
Math	Acute triangle	Obtuse triangle	List of grievances	Why we can't get along

Blogging can be used in any discipline to get kids exploring essential questions, investigating problems, or pondering discipline-specific topics in a safe (and engaging) space.

soared since initiating the practice, even though many of the tasks were ones students in the past may have groaned about completing with pen and paper. Students are also writing more since they are experiencing the satisfaction of writing for (and receiving feedback from) an authentic audience. Karen said, "I overheard three boys in my class comparing how many views they had on their blogs. There were 57, 80, and 114, respectively. The kid with only 57 was bummed, but I was excited!"

Blogging can be used in any discipline to get kids exploring essential questions, investigating problems, or pondering discipline-specific topics in a safe (and engaging) space that mirrors the habits of those in the field.

How It Works

Since Karen has been using blogs for several years with her students, she has worked out many of the kinks that get in the way of using this innovative tool with students. Figure 3.9 shows an adapted handout Karen provides to students to help them write their blogs.

Figure 3.9

Tips for Writing Interesting Blogs

- Create visual interest

  o Design your blog to reflect your personality. You don't have to restrict yourself to the available templates.

  o Use widgets if you want, but use them sparingly and with a purpose in mind. Don't clutter your blog unnecessarily.

  o Use images and videos, but don't steal these from other sites. Be aware of copyright issues. There are a variety of ways to find images and videos that you have permission to use. (Check with librarians as your school may pay for licenses for these resources.)

- Use a conversational tone. Try to interest the reader from the beginning.

- Use stories to relate common experiences that you and your readers might share.

- If you are a humorous person, use humor. (If this is not your style, that's okay.)

- Develop that habit of curating things that you run across or think about that might relate to your topic. (Tools such as Diigo or Evernote are good for this.)

- Your blog should be long enough to make your point, but don't overdo it. Remember that your writing should always be interesting.

- Think before you write and allow yourself to compose your entry over a period of time rather than in one session.

- Compose your entry in an offline document and then cut/paste into your online blog.

- Link to other resources and content. If you reference something you read on another blog, link to that blog and give the blogger credit.

- Read and comment on other people's blogs.

- Use a catchy title as "click bait" for your posts. It's fun to get readers from outside the classroom.

Source: Contributed by Karen Castelli.

Grading Student Blogs

Karen uses a rubric to evaluate the quality of the student's posts, but she makes sure students understand that she will not comment on every entry every week. She does, however, require students to reply to any comments that she or classmates make.

The following self-reflection tool developed by Karen helps guide students in their writing:

- Did you fully explain the concepts, terms, or ideas from class?
- Did you give a unique example or application, not an example from class?
- Did you properly refer to multiple sources from class?
- Did you explain the sources' connection to sociology in your own words?
- Did you explain the connection using your own words and referring to a source you found on your own?

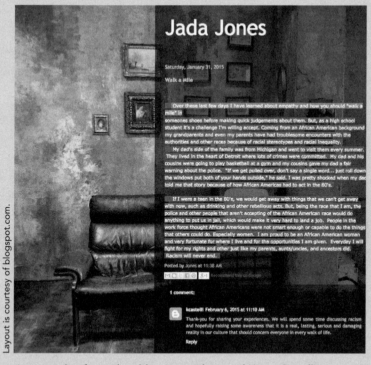

Layout is courtesy of blogspot.com.

An example of a student blog in sociology and Karen Castelli's response.

Ideas for Using Blogs in Various Disciplines

- Ask students to find photographs to post and then have students respond to them creatively in ELA, analytically in science or math, or in an interpretive manner in social studies.

- Have students use blogs as publications for research or projects.

- When students create RAFT writings (see page 96), have them post their creations as blogs and respond to each other's ideas online.

- Hold blog discussions instead of conducting whole-class oral discussions.

- Use blogs as places for students to write reflective pieces after completing a project or experiment, solving a problem, or reading a text.

- Give students mentor texts from your discipline and ask them to mimic the style, organization, or voice of the writer in their blog.

- Have students use blogs to explore social justice or current events issues. Many times such discussions evolve into long-term, thought-provoking writing that students wish to publish elsewhere.

Why It Works

Blogging works for obvious reasons: It provides students with the opportunity to interact with an authentic audience that offers immediate feedback. The collaborative nature of this activity also encourages intrinsic motivation, often flowing into out-of-school literacies that hook students in ways traditional classroom study simply can't. Karen has observed the following advantages of student blogging. She finds that her students

- Move away from concerns about their "grade" as they become interested in a wider audience for their ideas

- Establish an academic community where they enjoy engaging with and learning from each other

- Increase their metacognitive skills as they compare their level of thinking and writing with those of their classmates; she says blogging promotes more realistic self-assessment

- Blossom in a safe environment, especially introverted students or those who lack the self-efficacy to engage in other classroom activities

Extend and Adapt

Work with a teacher from another (or the same) discipline, school, or space across the world in partnering classes to blog with each other regarding similar topics. If that isn't feasible, then place students in blog groups within the class for specific assignments, using the tool as an interactive place for online composing and creating.

George Hillocks, Jr. (1995), a professor who spent his long career exploring the difficulties and rewards of writing in the classroom, argued that writing cannot be defined as correct spelling or structurally perfect paragraphs devoid of meaningful content. He often said in his succinct manner that writing is the production of meaning. Students who write within the content areas learn to produce meaning in discipline-specific ways that reach past formulaic organizers, traits for writing, writing strategies, or even the activities suggested in this chapter (which are intended as scaffolds to in-depth content-area writing). The most important consideration for content-area writing is that students employ the habits of mind that experts in the field have developed (see Chapter 4, pages 118–121). Student writing must move from exercises about the content to authenticity within the content: writing that evaluates, defends, questions, constructs, and creates.

Making it Relevant

1. How many different ways of writing can you identify in your discipline? How often do you use each of these ways of writing in a two-week period? A grading period?

2. How difficult will it be for you let go of the idea that you must grade all writing? How will you change your writing assessment practices based on what you've read in this chapter?

3. What one writing activity that you've read about in this chapter can you adapt to meet your needs?

Notes:

Suggestions for Further Reading

The Best-Kept Teaching Secret: How Written Conversations Engage Kids, Activate Learning, Grow Fluent Writers . . . K–12 by Harvey Daniels and Elaine Daniels, 2013.

Literacy Lessons for a Digital World: Using Blogs, Wikis, Podcasts, and More to Meet the Demands of the Common Core by Jamie E. Diamond and Meg C. Gaier Knapik, 2014.

Minds Made for Stories: How We Really Read and Write Informational and Persuasive Texts by Thomas Newkirk, 2014.

The Neglected "R": The Need for A Writing Revolution by the National Commission on Writing in America's Schools and Colleges, The College Board (http://www.collegeboard.com/prod_downloads/writingcom/neglectedr.pdf), 2003.

Write for Mathematics by Andrew S. Rothstein, Evelyn B. Rothstein, and Gerald Lauber, 2006.

Writing Instruction That Works: Proven Methods for Middle and High School Classrooms by Arthur N. Applebee and Judith A. Langer, 2013.

Writing Now: An NCTE Research Policy Brief by the National Council of Teachers of English, 2008.

CHAPTER

4

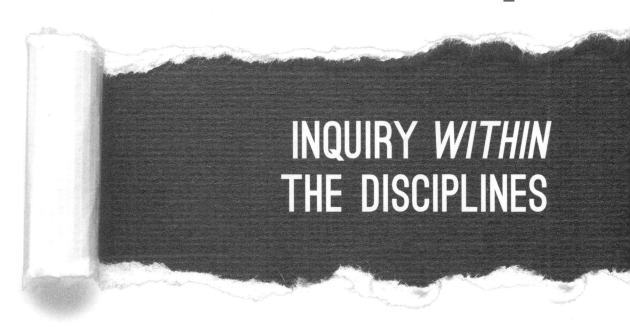

INQUIRY *WITHIN* THE DISCIPLINES

Students in Mr. Dykema's economics class became frustrated when he repeatedly responded to their questions with more questions and refused to neither confirm nor deny their theories about a bull market. "Why do you think that event would create such a market?" "How does your theory differ from Garrett's?" "Can you point to a time in history when economists agreed with you?" he asked.

Finally, one student, not quite under her breath, said, "Why don't you just tell us what you want us to know?" Ben Dykema looked up from where he was working with a small group and said, equally softly, "Because I want you to learn."

Inquiry and Disciplinary Literacy

Inquiry is at the core of learning in all disciplines. The complex attributes used to make sense of information, such as strategic thinking, creativity, and insightfulness, are all based in inquiry. Curiosity and persistence, effects of inquiry, then sustain understandings in ways that strengthen content learning. What's more, we know that students who engage in robust, intricate thinking acquire knowledge in ways that allow them to make connections, use knowledge for intrinsic purposes and expand learning through talk, writing, and multiple texts.

One remarkable characteristic of inquiry is that it is done *by* the individual, not *to* the individual, and this active form of learning (advocated by both 21st Century Learning Initiatives and the Common Core) is what makes knowledge stick. As proof, a recent study found that the students of teachers who focus heavily on inquiry-based instruction significantly outperformed students who had received traditional instruction (Roth, Marshall, Taylor, Wilson, & Hvidsten, 2014).

Solving challenging problems, asking questions, and thinking about what and why we know invite a deep internalization that goes far beyond memorizing information for tests or learning for purposes set by the teacher. When students become habitual inquirers, they develop intrinsic motivation and learn to think strategically about core academic concepts, much as the students at the beginning of the chapter were doing in their economics class.

Shifts for Implementing Inquiry Within the Disciplines

Moving from a transmission model to an inquiry-based classroom does have its challenges, no doubt about that. Teachers often feel overwhelmed with classroom management issues as well as with the logistical underpinnings required for organization and sustainability.

Perhaps most challenging of all, students must have sufficient content knowledge in order to engage in inquiry. As some critics of inquiry-based learning have pointed out, students can't construct meaningful questions if they lack background knowledge or basic information regarding a topic. That means that teachers must know what information their students need and then provide just enough to ignite inquiry without giving so much that students' curiosity is doused.

The Next Generation Science Standards address this conundrum brilliantly in one of the three dimensions that they believe are needed to provide students with a high quality science education. We would do well to incorporate this dimension into other standards: "It is impossible to teach all the ideas related to a given discipline in exhaustive detail during the K–12 years. But given the cornucopia of information available today virtually at a touch—people live, after all, in an information age—an important role of science education is not to teach all the facts but rather to prepare students with sufficient core knowledge so that they can later acquire additional information on their own" (National Academy of Sciences, 2013, p. 2).

Take a look at the shifts in the shaded box on page 106 that help facilitate such a change, and identify those that are doable as you begin to move toward a more inquiry-based, student-centered classroom.

Just as with reading and writing, it is counterproductive to impose strategies for generic inquiry because the processes for inquiry are different in each discipline. Let's look at how those differences might manifest themselves in the four major disciplines.

Perhaps most challenging of all is that students must have sufficient content knowledge in order to engage in inquiry.

Inquiry Within Science

The well-known scientific method begins with a scientific question, uses appropriate systems to gather data, and then seeks evidence to form explanations and arguments. Since the method is prompted by inquiry, it may also be recursive, depending upon the outcomes. The

Shifts for Implementing Inquiry Within the Disciplines

Brent Peters and Joe Franzen

A student works on an interdisciplinary inquiry project on raised-bed gardening.

- Move from working alone to collaborating with one or more colleagues, either in the same discipline or across disciplines. Middle school social studies teacher Tim Kramer and English language arts (ELA) teacher Michele Kandl co-teach; together they created the activity in Chapter 2, page 48, something they believe would not have happened had they been teaching alone. Many teachers cite the synergistic effect of co-teaching as a factor in successful inquiry learning as well as creating a more enjoyable and productive environment.

- Put "coverage" on the back burner and don't expect to teach all the facts. Focus instead on pure learning and how students will best retain that learning: by doing.

- Allow the inquiry process to move through its stages. Posing an interesting problem and providing lots of resources, for example, may not be enough for students to engage in deep understanding of a problem. It is critical to provide sufficient background information, allow students to investigate thoroughly, give opportunities for peer feedback, and encourage students to learn from their mistakes, all of which requires time—and often patience.

- Don't underestimate the importance of reflection. For example, have students keep a log during the process where they write not only what is happening but *how* and *why*. Teach them that reflecting on their learning is an important step in problem solving.

- Utilize formative assessment every step of the way and don't be afraid to change horses in the middle of the stream if something is not working.

- Teach mini-lessons to the entire class so you can talk to everyone at once about common issues and then allow students to return to work individually or in small groups.

- Think in terms of having students engage in practices rather than in learning discrete skills.

- See yourself as a coach as students learn and practice the moves. The apprenticeship model really works—and supports inquiry.

- Use examples and models from previous classes or have students in other classes (or schools) discuss their experiences or provide feedback. Consider using tools such as Skype to put students in touch with experts and others who may have something to offer.

Next Generation Science Standards put teeth into this process through performance expectations, which move teachers far beyond checklists of material to cover. The standards are clear in this regard: "As in all inquiry-based approaches to science teaching, our expectation is that students will themselves engage in the practices and not merely learn about them secondhand. Students cannot comprehend scientific practices, nor fully appreciate the nature of scientific knowledge itself, without directly experiencing those practices for themselves" (National Academy of Sciences, 2013, p. 2).

Jeff Marshall, author of *Succeeding with Inquiry in Science and Math Classrooms* (2013), argues that the reason for the inclusion of inquiry in the new standards is obvious when looking at the significant advantages in inquiry instruction: It provides opportunities to more easily differentiate instruction, fosters mastery of higher-order thinking, and reduces student apathy (p. 19).

In explaining the process of inquiry, consider how a geologist might engage in the scientific method when he discovers a grove of dead cedar trees on a shoreline. He will probably

- Make observations

- Use curiosity and background knowledge to define questions

- Gather evidence using technology and mathematics

- Utilize previous research

- Propose a possible explanation

- Publish an explanation based on evidence

- Consider new evidence

- Add to his explanation

- Use his explanation to inform public policy (Olson & Loucks-Horsley, 2000).

Inquiry in science means that students learn to do science in place of learning about science.

While I may repeat myself on this point, it is a point worth repeating: Inquiry in science means that students learn to *do* science in place of learning *about* science.

Science teachers who know their content spend less time having students read information from textbooks and more time employing powerful forms of inquiry to build deep and lasting understanding.

Inquiry Within History and Social Studies

Historical inquiry is based on the examination of primary documents with questions as the guiding force in the reading. As Anita Ravi (2010) notes, "The job of the historian is to sift through the fragments that history leaves behind to create a narrative of what happened" (p. 35). Historians typically approach texts with a specific purpose for reading, almost always based in inquiry as they seek an explanation or interpretation of a significant historical incident, analyze cause and effect, or reconstruct an event. They work to ask the right questions, find reliable sources, and accurately comprehend texts, while comparing and contrasting perspectives, making inferences, and grappling with multifaceted inquiries such as the following:

Colleen Zenner and Justin Stroh

High school students engaged in inquiry in Colleen Zenner and Justin Stroh's science class.

- What really happened at the Boston Massacre?

- How did Martin Luther King create a movement and what might have happened had he not been assassinated?

- What part did Rasputin play in the death of the Romanovs during the Russian Revolution?

- Is torture ever justified?

- How does the US policy regarding ISIS differ from that of other countries?

- How might historical accounts related in textbooks be incorrect from a single perspective? You might have students read sections of *Lies My Teacher Told Me: Everything Your American History Book Got Wrong* (Loewen, 2007) to increase curiosity.

Compare this active approach to the traditional one of reading a chapter and memorizing details of a historical event, and it's clear that all learning is not the same. If we want students to know how to interrogate texts rather than simply read them, we have to teach them to act as historians who can effectively uncover answers and draw conclusions as they learn to engage fully in the process of historical study.

Inquiry is actually a perfect fit for all social studies courses, especially since controversial issues are often discussed in this discipline. (See Chapter 2, pages 33–37, for activities related to current events.) Debates, mock trials, forums, social justice projects, and argumentative essays all begin with inquiry. Help students' inquisitive juices begin flowing by sending them to sites such as procon.org, *New York Times* Learning Network blog *Room for Debate* column, and Tolerance.org.

We want students to know how to interrogate texts rather than simply read them—to act as historians who can effectively uncover answers and draw conclusions.

Inquiry Within Math

Just as with the other disciplines, inquiry in math calls for a specific mindset based on habits of thinking that support the reasoning required to do math.

Math instruction in earlier years relied on a very limited type of inquiry, often called prescriptive inquiry, where students were led through problems with a clear and definitive answer, more of a "follow the rules" to "find the right answer" approach.

Today, mathematical inquiry is based on process as well as proficiency and may require broader skills such as the following:

- Questioning and investigating patterns

- Applying previously learned mathematical skills to new problems or real-world events

- Finding connections between graphs, charts, and other texts through mathematical principles and applications

- Engaging in estimation and conjecture while tackling complex ideas, even if the answer is "wrong"

- Discovering generalizations and exceptions

- Recognizing the value in metacognitive activities, such as understanding and explaining thinking

- Working beside someone with advanced skills

Inquiry in math calls for a specific mindset based on habits of thinking that support the reasoning required to do math.

In an article titled "Uncovering the Math Curriculum," Marilyn Burns (2014) says, "I've come to realize that our challenge as teachers is not to find better ways to explain to our students what we want them to learn, but rather to find better ways to ask our students to make sense of what they're learning for themselves" (p. 64). She goes on to say that we should be encouraging students to ask "Why do we do this?" or "Why does this make sense?" For example, students might ask, "Why does canceling zeros produce an equivalent fraction in the fraction 10/20 but not in the fraction 101/201?" (p. 67). Such questions ground inquiry into the mathematical discipline.

Even in this discipline, one that has in the past been textbook heavy, we know that students must go beyond the abundant math problems in textbooks to develop an inquiry mindset.

Inquiry Within ELA

Many teachers of English were, themselves, taught in the transmission style. They completed study guides, often answering hundreds of low-level questions for one novel as they returned to highlighted passages in an effort to comprehend what the author said. For her part, the teacher explained what the author meant, as students took notes from lectures and engaged in whole-class discussions designed to promote "correct" thinking about the text. *Inquiry* was defined by the ubiquitous research paper, which was more about learning how to create a proper outline, cite sources correctly, and adhere to a certain organizational style than about genuine inquiry.

With a deeper learning emphasis comes a new meaning to ELA inquiry: Learners must explore multiple texts and compare perspectives, analyze and expand on concepts presented by authors, and learn to question ideas through various critical lenses. Inquiry in ELA, as opposed to other disciplines, may produce few concrete answers. The process of wondering, formulating questions, and thinking through concepts while respecting multiple viewpoints is as much the goal as certitude about a concept.

Speaking and listening are also components of inquiry in ELA classrooms as students engage in book clubs, seminars, and debates. They use both informational text and fiction to develop deep understanding of texts, elaborate on their own ideas, often initially through writing and, as a significant bonus, come to find enjoyment in multiple literacies.

What might inquiry in an ELA classroom look like?

- Students read widely from multiple sources to gain varied perspectives and learn to question the motivation behind those perspectives.

- Dialogue may take the form of seminars, inquiry circles, or debates rather than a whole-class discussion led by the teacher.

- Essential questions drive reading, writing, and discussion in place of preset text choices or a textbook's table of contents.

- Autonomy is afforded students in research, reading, writing, and performance as a way of sparking engagement and sustaining inquiry.

- Webquests for authentic audiences based on relevant questions supplant research papers for teachers' eyes only.

- Students learn to ask questions of the author and each other as they seek to uncover meaning in fiction or bias in nonfiction.

The ELA curriculum is quickly changing as teachers incorporate social and digital literacies into what was once a fixed, print-centric curriculum. Such engaging mediums, however, still require inquiry-based practices to help students become discerning, independent readers, writers, and thinkers.

The process of wondering, formulating questions, and thinking through concepts while respecting multiple viewpoints is as much the goal as certitude about a concept.

Questions (and Answers) About Inquiry Within the Disciplines

How can students engage in inquiry if they have little knowledge about the subject? Isn't it the teachers' job to provide the type of learning that may be considered "passive" in order to give students the information they need to begin the process of inquiry?

Students do need background information or at least some knowledge on which to build their inquiry. Inquiry-based teaching doesn't mean that kids are sent out as explorers to find the New World; it means, rather, that the teacher's role moves from one who parcels out information to one who guides learning based on her own expertise and ability to mentor students in their "doing."

Heather Banchi and Randy Bell discuss four levels of inquiry that may help teachers as they struggle with the "too little" or "too much" teaching dilemma. While their work (see the box on the facing page) is targeted toward science, the model of inquiry that they propose is useful for teachers of all disciplines as they think about their specific goals for instruction.

See the shaded box on page 114 for an example of how the levels of inquiry might look in an ELA class studying a poet such as T. S. Eliot.

When we view learning as a messy, recursive process, not a packaged product to be unwrapped and consumed, we know that "incorrect conclusions" can be used by good teachers to help students develop transformative understandings in their discipline.

What if students spend a long time engaged in inquiry and then come up with incorrect conclusions? How can I justify the time spent?

A quick Google search reveals hundreds of initial "incorrect conclusions" that eventually led to life-changing advances in all sorts of fields. The discovery of penicillin may be the most valuable "failure" followed, some would contend, by the Post-it Note. Thomas Edison's many failed attempts to create a light bulb filament before he became successful is also high on the list. And Albert Einstein was fond of failure as well, saying, "I have not failed. I have just found 10,000 ways that won't work."

Banchi and Bell's Four Levels of Inquiry

1. **Confirmation Inquiry:** Students are provided with the question and method, but the teacher expects that students will determine a result (or answer) that is known in advance. This type of inquiry may be beneficial if teachers want to review or reinforce learning—or introduce students to the inquiry process.

2. **Structured Inquiry:** Students are provided with the question and method, but in this case, students generate the explanation for the evidence they have uncovered. This process may be useful for scaffolding more independent inquiry as students build new understandings in content areas.

3. **Guided Inquiry:** Students are provided with the research question, but they must design the method and resulting explanations. An advantage of this type of inquiry is that it allows the teacher to engage in differentiated instruction and targeted assessment.

   Note that students should have numerous opportunities for participating in inquiry-based learning before they engage in guided inquiry.

4. **Open Inquiry:** Students have opportunities to act as experts in the field. They derive questions, design and conduct investigations, and communicate their results. Clearly, this is the most cognitively challenging stage of inquiry, but it also derives the most benefits in terms of independent learning and deep understanding.

Source: Adapted from Banchi & Bell, 2008.

Admittedly, most of our students are not going to become future Einsteins or Edisons. The principle, nevertheless, holds true. When we view learning as a messy, recursive process, not a packaged product to be unwrapped and consumed, we know that "incorrect conclusions" can be used by good teachers to help students develop transformative understandings in their discipline.

It can be very difficult for us to embrace failure, especially when it seems as though our students are making mistakes that we can correct. Diana Laufenberg in her TED Talk discusses the importance of allowing students to learn from failure. It's worth viewing and discussing within your PLC (www.ted.com/talks/diana_laufenberg_3_ways_to_teach#).

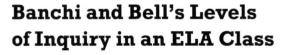

Banchi and Bell's Levels of Inquiry in an ELA Class

- **Confirmation Inquiry:** After introducing students to a few poems by T. S. Eliot, an ELA teacher may want students to uncover the meaning in one of his more challenging poems, say "The Love Song of J. Alfred Prufrock." She might ask the question, "In what way, if any, is this poem autobiographical?" and then provide students with a short biography of Eliot's life, expecting that students would be able to point out areas in which the poem is autobiographical based on their new reading.

- **Structured Inquiry:** Using the same T. S. Eliot poem, students might be asked, "Why is the poem 'The Love Song of J. Alfred Prufrock' a 'love song'?" Students might then be provided with a text about Eliot's relationship to Rudyard Kipling as well as Kipling's poem "The Love Song of Har Dyal," which influenced Eliot's work. After reading both texts, students would be expected to provide an answer (or explanation) to the question, using their reading as evidence.

- **Guided Inquiry:** In using the same Eliot poem referenced above, the teacher will now provide a research question such as "In what way is the poem 'The Love Song of Alfred J. Prufrock' an example of stream of consciousness style of writing?" Students will find resources that help them answer the question beginning with research on the stream of consciousness technique and then formulate an answer, citing examples from the poem.

- **Open Inquiry:** For this type of inquiry, students would read our Eliot poem several times with a teacher as well as independently or with a learning partner. They would be asked to come up with questions related to the poem that would help other readers gain understanding of his complex ideas. Students would investigate possible answers to the questions, and then share their findings with a small group or the whole class.

And, a final point. How many students have written incorrect information on a test after weeks of instruction, accepted their grade without question, and never had a chance to use their efforts at learning to find a correct solution or develop understanding? Learning through inquiry may take longer than learning through transmission, but if we want deep learning instead of superficial coverage, it's worth the investment.

Spotlight on ELA and Technology

Contributed by Bill Seidel, digital-age-learning coach; Carrie Raia and Robin Padal, sixth-grade ELA teachers; and Jeanne Norgan, sixth-grade English language learner (ELL) teacher

The iPad makes the process of using inquiry to spark creative ideas simpler for most students. At our middle school, teachers combined their talents in English, ELL, and technology to produce a project that challenged students to uncover the concept of *successful failure* from their own experience or through the lens of a famous person. Students read and analyzed multiple articles of resilient famous people from Albert Einstein to Taylor Swift in order to frame their perspective on the topic. Then, students wrote about how failure can be an important experience through an online class discussion forum where they could provide each other feedback on how they interpreted the reading.

Lauren Walker
Successful failure

Failure 3: Failed military entrance exam 3 times
01:26   02:19

Fri Feb 20, 2015 at 8:37 am · Like 👍 1 · Reply

Anne Davenport
Lauren, I like how you had a lot of information, and I like the pictures.
Mon Feb 23, 2015 at 8:30 am · Like · Reply

Heyu Sun
Lauren, your video is very informative and well organized. I really liked the speech your insert in the beginning. I learned he had a lot of failures but he also overcame all of them. For example, I learned Churchill had fail to get in the military. But he had a tutor and later became one of the famous military leader. Great job!
Mon Feb 23, 2015 at 8:32 am · Like · Reply

Jennifer Devona
Lauren, I learned that Churchill has long-term goals and endurance. I learned about his early life and how he was resilient and is now one of the most well known speakers! Good job!
Thu Mar 12, 2015 at 9:11 am · Like · Reply

Facebook

Students engage in an online class discussion forum about successful failures.

From there, students were challenged to produce an inspirational video allowing them to choose someone that embodied the value of overcoming failure in life. Their product had to be either a commercial, public service announcement, minidocumentary, or interview telling their subject's story while artfully pulling in terminology learned in class. To begin the creative process, students were first asked to recognize the differences in the various media types. Next, students planned out their concept in a research organizer and storyboard as they picked their subject and teased out the direction of the video.

In the end, students used various applications to build a successful iMovie video. In order to create an authentic audience, students posted their videos to an online forum where their classmates and teachers could give them feedback and praise. As a result of this personal study, students continue to recognize successful failure occurring in the world around them and in the literature they read, frequently bringing stories in to share.

I find several models for inquiry-based learning in professional materials. How do I know which one works best?

There is no one way to engage in inquiry-based learning. It takes the professional judgment of the teacher, preferably in collaboration with colleagues, perhaps through lesson study or dialogue, to come up with the best way to use inquiry for your discipline, topic, and students. In *Common Core CPR: What About Adolescents Who Struggle . . . or Just Don't Care?* (2013), my coauthor Barry Gilmore and I developed a model for problem-based learning. The important thing to remember is that problem- or project-based learning has its roots in inquiry, usually focused on a specific problem. Our model, similar to others, follows these steps:

- Provide an anchor that offers background to generate interest.
- Give students choice in some aspect of the project.
- Generate a problem statement or driving questions.
- Provide opportunities for students to raise questions, become familiar with the problem, and explore multiple facets of the issue.
- Teach students to conduct rigorous investigation.
- Help students analyze findings and draw conclusions.
- Provide ongoing feedback and revision from teachers and peers.

- Engage in reflection.

- Assess in authentic ways (Lent & Gilmore, 2013, pp. 168–169).

Figure 4.1 shows how a science class and an ELA class approached project-based learning with an action component.

Figure 4.1

Project-Based Learning Activities in ELA and Science

What causes bullying? What can we do about it in our school?	What is composting? How can we compost scraps from the school's cafeteria?
Anchor: • Read about recent school shootings or incidents of bullying in the news. • In small groups, relate personal experiences about bullying. • Read informational texts about bullying. • Read young adult novels about bullying.	**Anchor:** • Read general articles about the process of composting. • Watch videos on composting. • Interview expert on composting (guest speaker).
Inventory: • What do students know? • How do they feel about this topic? • What do we want them to know? • What do we want them to learn by doing?	**Inventory:** • What do students know? • What do we know them to know? • What do we want them learn by doing?

(Continued)

(Continued)

What causes bullying? What can we do about it in our school?	What is composting? How can we compost scraps from the school's cafeteria?
Choice: Students choose an incident of bullying to research: causes and repercussions	**Choice:** Choose one aspect of composting to research: • materials • process • containers • cafeteria food waste
Activities: Reading, researching, writing, discussing, interviewing, sharing information	**Activities:** Field trips, interviewing, reading, researching, writing, keeping logs, sharing information
Drawing Conclusions: What are the causes of bullying?	**Drawing Conclusions:** How can we create a plan for composting scraps from the cafeteria?
Action: In small groups, create a plan that may reduce bullying in school.	**Action:** Construct a composting area or bin near the cafeteria and a plan for its use.
Implementation: Class representative meets with principal to discuss implementation of plan.	**Implementation:** Share information about new composting site with media, local gardeners, and others.

There is a lot of talk about "habits of mind." What, exactly, are these habits and why are they important? Is this one more thing I will be required to incorporate into my content area?

Habits of mind, or the term I prefer, *habits of thinking*, are integral to inquiry and to each discipline because thoughtful, intelligent, successful people exhibit certain dispositions when they address complex problems, and we want students to practice and develop these dispositions as well. One of the advantages of inquiry-based learning is that students don't just learn how to solve one problem or think through one complex situation; instead, as they engage in inquiry, they develop habits (skills, attitudes, past experiences) that will transfer to other disciplines and other problems.

In other words, students learn how to think about their own thinking as they engage in something concrete that focuses their learning. That's why it's worth the time to invest in inquiry; students learn more than we can possibly teach them in a traditional sit-and-get environment.

While there are several approaches to habits of mind, Arthur Costa and Bena Kallick's (2009) work in habits of mind is comprehensive and applicable to the inquiry method used by most educators. In Chapter 2 from the excellent book *Deeper Learning: Beyond 21st Century Skills* (Bellanca, 2015), the authors emphasize the importance of dispositions of learning.

> Authoritative futurists, neuroscientists, educators, and sociologists cite the need for problem solving, creating, innovating, and communicating to sustain the democratic and capitalistic society in which we live. The authors use different terms, but they all reference dispositions that are necessary to lend oneself to learning. In the absence of these dispositions, students will be unable to become productive, innovative, problem solvers for our economy and for our democracy. (pp. 56–57)

Students don't just learn how to solve one problem or think through one complex situation; instead, as they engage in inquiry, they develop habits that will transfer to other disciplines and other problems.

One of the best way to help students recognize and develop such dispositions is to ask them to come up with their own lists of habits for your discipline and add them to the chart's first column in Figure 4.2, an adaptation of Costa and Kallick's *Habits of Mind*. Figure 4.2 also offers an active way to help kids make a connection from their own learning to habits of thinking exhibited by experts in the field. Be sure and explain to students what each of the characteristics might look like in your discipline. You might also ask students to write about their learning experiences in order to gain a

Figure 4.2

Self-Reflection Survey: Habits of Mind Adapted From Costa and Kallick

For this project or task, rate your habits of mind:

Habit	I did not exhibit this habit very well. Explain.	My ability to engage in this habit was about average for me.	I did a good job of exhibiting this habit. Provide an example.	Not applicable to this task or project.
Showed persistence				
Managed my impulsivity				
Listened with understanding and empathy				
Thought about my thinking				
Engaged in flexible thinking				
Valued accuracy				
Questioned and posed problems				
Applied past knowledge to this project or task				
Gathered information through all my senses				
Engaged in curiosity and enthusiasm				
Took responsible risks				
Found humor				
Thought independently				
Remained open to new and continuous learning				
Used my abilities to create, imagine, and innovate				
Thought and communicated with clarity and precision				

conceptual understanding of the terms before they begin an inquiry project and certainly before completing the survey. Notice that not all habits are appropriate for all projects or tasks, so use this template as model to design your own.

Consider asking students to devote a page in their learning logs to "Habits of Mind" or use another phrase such as "What do I think I'm doing?" to monitor their own thinking processes as they become involved in the work of your discipline.

One of the messiest parts of inquiry learning to me is the assessment. How do I assess inquiry so that my evaluation isn't so subjective?

The best assessment for inquiry learning is formative since inquiry is a process that does not always lead to a quantifiable product.

And when a product, demonstration, or presentation (such as a newscast, video, infographic, or essay) is the final outcome, you have an opportunity to use a summative assessment that isn't pen and paper.

But here's the most exciting point. When intrinsic motivation, one of the most important goals of inquiry, is developed, there is little need to continually assess because students will generally go beyond your expectations. Often, giving students participation grades during the process is enough to make sure they are involved in the activity, especially when they engage in discussion or questioning. You may also utilize the quickjots described in Chapter 3 (page 92) to monitor learning.

Consider individual conferences as checkpoints, as well, where you monitor students' electronic or paper portfolios as they place or record work in progress as well as their reflections of learning. In the spirit of independent inquiry, provide check-in sheets (see Figure 4.3) that students must complete prior to meeting with you for the conference. As always, place the responsibility for inquiry directly on students and ask that they demonstrate to you what and how they are learning.

The best assessment for inquiry learning is formative since inquiry is a process that does not always lead to a quantifiable product.

Figure 4.3

Conference Check-in Planning Sheet (to be completed by student)

Answer each question to the best of your ability prior to your conference. Have examples ready to show and be prepared to take notes as we discuss your project.

1. What work do you want to show me during this conference?

2. What progress have you made on your learning (or project) since you last conferenced with me?

3. What problems are you having with your project or learning? How do you plan to address these problems?

4. What are your plans for the next phase of the project?

5. Is there anything else you want me to know about your project, your collaboration with others, or your learning so far?

I always have a couple of students—sometimes more than a couple—who simply won't participate in inquiry-based learning. They do as little as possible, often wasting their own time and the time of anyone else they are working with. In fact, they don't seem to be curious about much of anything school related. How do I get such students to care?

For some reason, some students are turned off to school, perhaps because of negative experiences in the past, a cultural bias against succeeding in school, or because they believe they are incapable of accomplishing the tasks we ask of them. In *Common Core CPR: What About Adolescents Who Struggle . . . or Just Don't Care?* (2013), my coauthor and I provide "standards" for motivation and engagement that you might find helpful. We found that relevance and autonomy often make a huge difference.

Caroline Milne

Science teacher Caroline Milne confers with a student about his project.

Another conceptual change approach to learning that involves relevance as a factor in motivation was developed by Marcia Linn, Elizabeth Davis, and Philip Bell (2004), referred to as the scaffolded knowledge integration framework, and may have a positive impact on students with low motivation—on all learners, actually. It was designed specifically for science, but its application fits right in with our disciplinary discussion on engagement and inquiry.

1. **Make science accessible:** Build on student ideas, provide personally relevant examples

2. **Make thinking visible:** Model scientific thinking, scaffold students to make their thinking visible, provide multiple representations

3. **Help students learn from others:** Encourage listening to others, design discussions, highlight cultural norms

4. **Promote autonomy and lifelong learning:** Encourage monitoring, provide complex projects, revisit and generalize inquiry processes, scaffold critique

Instead of beginning with the topic of the inquiry itself, use the components of the scaffolded integrated framework to set the stage for motivation by asking yourself the following:

- Do students have some input into the topic?

- In what way is the topic relevant to students' lives or interests?

- Have I provided enough scaffolding and modeling to hook students?

- Are there sufficient opportunities for students to be heard, even those who are resistant?

- Do students feel they have autonomy in the inquiry?

My bet is that the students who refuse to participate aren't getting much from a traditional lecture-read-fill-in-the-blanks approach either. Sometimes the best we can do is provide opportunities for rich learning for everyone and hope that those who aren't interested will eventually be drawn in—despite themselves.

How to Get Students Inquiring Within the Disciplines

1. THINKING AS A SKEPTIC

Students who think about information with a questioning eye learn to use inquiry in ways that will benefit them for life. Turn your class into a group of intellectual skeptics through the following activity.

How It Works

First, be on the lookout for texts with embedded bias, such as examples from the following list:

- Advertisements or commercials

- Websites that advocate a certain position (such as www.friendsofcoal.org and www.nature.org)

- Op-ed pieces or blogs on topics related to your discipline

- Pieces that use numbers or data, such as *Harper's Index*

- Book or movie reviews

- YouTube clips of someone advocating a position

- Political cartoons, speeches, or debates

Place students into small groups. You may provide to each group different versions of the same text or give everyone the exact same text. Ask them to use the graphic organizer in Figure 4.4 to think about the message skeptically.

Figure 4.4

The Skeptic Ponders a Text

What does the text say?	What does the text mean?
What has the author or creator omitted that should have been included?	**What would I like to ask the creators or authors of the text?**
What evidence have I found to support the author's statements?	**What evidence have I found to refute the author's statements?**

Why It Works

Too many students have been taught to accept what they are reading as fact. Many students, despite being naturally oppositional, don't quarrel with the text because accepting what is in print (or online) and answering a few questions require little thinking. They can buy into a simple formula: read, remember, and regurgitate (the 3 *R*s of high-stakes testing). Once they learn how to think like a skeptic, however, they begin to form an inquiry mindset—reading and viewing with skepticism instead of with nods. This approach is the precursor to the skills advocated by virtually all standards: evaluation of texts, determination of credibility and accuracy, and critical thinking.

Extend and Adapt

Help students learn how to think skeptically by turning the tables. Explain some of the most common logical fallacies such as slippery slope, straw man, or bandwagon. Take a look at *An Illustrated Book of Bad Arguments* (Almossawi, 2014) to engage students in nineteen common errors in reasoning along with humorous visuals that illustrate the fallacy. You may want to divide students into small groups, assign one of the fallacies for them to study, and have them present examples of their assigned fallacy to the rest of the class as a background-building activity.

Then, have students use at least one of the fallacies to create a cartoon, advertisement, or op-ed piece. Students will exchange their pieces and use "The Skeptic Ponders a Text" chart (Figure 4.4) to analyze their peer's piece.

2. PLAYING THE PHILADELPHIA LAWYER

Just as students must develop fluency in reading and writing, they must also develop fluency in inquiry or thinking curiously.

How It Works

The groundwork should be laid for this activity, specifically through activities that show students what good questions look like.

Asking Good Questions

Provide mentor texts that show the power of good questions in prompting thinking (as well as interesting answers). *Time* magazine's "Answers Issue" (time.com/the-answers-issue) offers questions that can't help but elicit thinking, such as

- Why doesn't the heart get cancer?

- What is the most patriotic color?

- How safe are you from a natural disaster?

- Why does the bag on the airplane not inflate if oxygen is flowing to the mask?

Also check out the compelling book *What If? Serious Scientific Answers to Absurd Hypothetical Questions* (Munroe, 2014) where the questions are as challenging as the answers. Other books such as *Why Rattlesnakes Rattle . . . and 250 Other Things You Should Know* (Helterbran, 2012) provide endless questions to get kids thinking in the interrogative mode.

Students may still need some guidelines for creating their own questions. The following tips may be helpful, but ask students to contribute to the list as well.

Good questions

- Create excitement by pulling readers into the question, making them so curious they can't wait to find out the answer

- May have more than one answer or no answer at all; some questions are designed to prompt thinking or make a point instead of seeking an answer

- Rarely have black-and-white answers and always require more than a simple yes or no answer

- Are not designed to stump or trick the person who is attempting to answer— or to put him down or make him feel stupid

- Are specific and clear

- Don't seek to move the answerer into a defensive position

- Prompt deep, sometimes transformative, thinking

Questioning the Text

Give students a piece of text that leaves room for questions. For example, an article from the *New York Times* (which, interestingly begins with the question "Why Is Measles So Contagious?")—complete with a graph and chart—discusses the measles outbreak, how an infected person spreads the virus, and how many people die from the disease. Such an article should garner plenty of questions, especially because of its relevance (www.nytimes.com/interactive/2015/02/02/us/measles-facts.html?ref=us&_r=0).

The following is an activity related to the article about measles that can be adapted to many other texts.

1. Have students read the article and come up with three "good" questions individually, such as the following:

   - Which other viruses are airborne?
   - How soon does the rash appear after someone has been infected?
   - Why are people getting the measles if there is a vaccine?

2. Students will share their questions in a small group and, together, come up with one "best" question.

3. One student from each group will write the group's question on the whiteboard.

4. Group members will come to consensus on one of the posted questions to research.

4. The group will share the researched answers with the class.

Why It Works

A 2014 study into curiosity and learning from the University of California found three important findings related to inquiry. First, when curiosity is present, people are better at learning information, especially when curiosity is presented as a question. Second, when curiosity is stimulated, there is increased brain activity associated with positive rewards. Amazingly, intrinsic motivation taps into the same brain areas that are associated with extrinsic motivation. And finally, the study reveals that curiosity allows the brain to retain information better than when curiosity is not present (Cell Press, 2014). The best part is that the study also shows that once curiosity is aroused, people could also better learn entirely unrelated information. Indeed, there seem to be no reasons *not* to utilize inquiry in all disciplines as often as possible.

Extend and Adapt

Have students think about why people create questions, even subconsciously, such as in gaming, to convey information, or as a rhetorical device. If it is an election year, show them a video of the questions that a moderator asks candidates in a televised presidential or gubernatorial debate, and have students analyze the questions in terms of effectiveness and then come up with follow-up questions they would like to ask. To help students develop a questioning mindset, have them turn statements into questions—such as headings in textbooks or headlines in news articles—and fine-tune their questioning skills by talking to people who make a living asking questions such as lawyers, detectives, and insurance investigators. Invite someone who uses questions as a basis for their work to talk to the class and ask them to discuss the characteristics of good questions as well as how questions drive their thinking.

3. SOLVING THE MYSTERY

A mystery is a hook for learning, and students will respond enthusiastically if they can act as investigators rather than as passive learners. It's just a matter of creating a bit of the clandestine in the classroom.

How It Works

Instead of telling students the main ideas in a topic of study, for instance, give them enough details to make them curious about "the rest of the story" and then allow them to use their powers of inquiry to figure it out, with engaging mini-lessons or chunks of information provided by the teacher. For example, in history when students read about the ruined South at the end of the Civil War, they could also be told that there were two very different opinions on how to reconstruct the South. What were these opinions? Which one makes the most sense? What happened, eventually?

A 2014 study into curiosity and learning from the University of California reveals that curiosity allows the brain to retain information better than when curiosity is not present.

Spotlight on ELA

Inquiry in ELA classes can often lead to full-blown projects, especially based on novels that leave the reader with more questions than answers. Amy Stewart, a middle school ELA teacher, had her students keep an inquiry log as they were reading and then develop three essential questions from the notes and queries in their log. They had to address the questions through research and writing. "Students surprised me with their questions," she said. "They seemed to delve much deeper into the book when they were asking questions rather than answering questions that I provided. The research regarding their questions was also more in depth, possibly because they had come up with the questions themselves."

Luci Dvorak, Colleen McWalter, and Dina Giannakopoulos, high school English teachers, used an inquiry approach when their freshman students read *Romeo and Juliet*. While students were reading the play, they generated an inquiry research question related to the idea of love. Students came up with questions such as "When does love become an obsession?" and "How do you know when you have found true love?" In groups, students had to find an answer to their inquiry question and include research from a movie, an interview, and an article. The interview and article had to be completed independently. Then, students took all of the research and created a presentation that answered their original question.

Luci had first come up with the idea when her students read Tim O'Brien's (2009) *The Things They Carried,* and she had them conduct research on veterans. She said the inquiry component not only made the experience more enjoyable for students but also deepened their understanding of the book. She cited the following evaluation of the project written by one of her students as an example. "The presentation helped me better understand the book. I concluded that people are constantly building upon themselves; their identities are frequently evolving. In addition, I learned a lot about myself in the process of preparing for this presentation. I also overcame my fear of speaking in front of my peers, which was one of my goals for this year."

This activity may seem easier in disciplines such as history and English, where stories are often embedded in content, but science and math contain stories as well. In science, a teacher might project photographs of a lake before and after the drought in California and ask students to come up with the rest of the story. A math teacher may give students two word problems and ask them how the problems are similar or differ, how the information could be shown in a chart or graph, and how many different ways students could find to solve the problems. They might then be asked to continue the story by creating another set of word problems that use the same process for finding the answer.

Why It Works

Why do television shows such as *CSI* work? People always want to know the rest of the story; it provides an almost impossible-to-resist hook. Even the college board has wised up to this truism for AP classes, and they are now revising their previous approach, which was one of overwhelming students with tremendous amounts of information to be memorized for a test. Their new position advocates reducing the breadth of content and focusing on conceptual understandings. Science, in particular, is moving solidly back to scientific inquiry and student-directed labs because, as we all know, every lab tells a story.

Extend and Adapt

There are many books for content-area subjects that can be used to help students engage in investigative thinking such as the following:

- *The Dark Game: True Spy Stories From Invisible Ink to CIA Moles* (2010) by Paul B. Janeczko offers a mesmerizing collection of spy stories from American history that prompt deep and creative thinking if used as what-happened-next scenarios.

- *Photo by Brady: A Picture of the Civil War* (2005) by Jennifer Armstrong presents real photographs of the Civil War. Ask students to create a story around a photograph, especially if they research the date and location of the photograph before beginning their story.

- *We Were Liars* (2014), a compelling young adult novel by E. Lockhart is told from the perspective an unreliable narrator with a mysterious twist at the end. Have students read the book and only write questions in their learning logs rather than responses or summaries. There are countless novels that could be used in this way to elicit inquisitive thinking in ELA.

- *Mathematical Curiosities: A Treasure Trove of Unexpected Entertainments* (2014) by Alfred Posamentier and Ingmar Lehmann makes math come alive through curiously interesting problems, information, and strange tidbits, such as how Babylonian peasants solved multiplications of large numbers.

- There are many young adult novels as well as nonfiction books addressing topics in science, especially with the explosion of science fiction writing. One that comes to mind is *Double Helix* (2005) by Nancy Werlin, a book of fiction about molecular biology and genetics, with a surprise around every corner. Students who have a grasp of the topic may be able to unravel the mystery before they get to the end of the book.

4. INTERVIEWING THE SUBJECT

Interviews have been a mainstay of inquiry in classrooms for many years, but in the technology age it takes on a new spin. No longer do students call for an appointment and then sit across the desk from an expert, notebook in lap. They can now reach out to just about anyone through communication tools such as Skype or e-mail, making it easier to focus on the interview itself.

How It Works

First, have students come up with a purpose for their interview, such as wanting to know what it was like to be in Vietnam during the 1960s, why the bee population is declining in a particular area, how math is used in investment banking, or how a particular young adult novelist came up with an idea for a recent book.

Provide students with ideas about where to find interviewees: colleges or universities, professional societies, groups (such as the Audubon Society), experts in the field who have blogs, Twitter accounts or websites, or businesses associated with the topic. Have students research at least two possible interviewees who might be able to answer their questions—or they might begin by researching the specialty fields or careers of the interviewee.

Students will then think about the medium they want to use to conduct the interview before contacting their interviewee. Remind students that their first choice of interviewee may not have the time or interest in being interviewed, so they may need to move on to their second choice.

Students should work in small groups to help each other develop thoughtful initial questions as well as appropriate follow-up questions, perhaps practicing with their learning partner. Students should have at least twenty questions, some of which they may not ask, so instruct them to place the questions in order of importance. You may want to have students turn in the interview questions so you can assess the quality of the questions. Some students, especially if they are new to this process, may need help developing appropriately in-depth questions to make the interview worthwhile.

After the interview, students will share their findings either through a written report, a visual, or a presentation within small groups or to the whole class.

Why It Works

Interview projects move active learning front and center, both in the classroom and outside of it. With this activity, students can synthesize and practice important literacy skills such as the following:

- Speaking, listening, and note-taking
- Reading and writing for authentic purposes
- Learning through various perspectives
- Assuming ownership of an activity

- Fostering independence
- Summarizing, inferring, and determining importance
- Learning how literacy is used in real world situations
- Developing academic communication skills

Extend and Adapt

Some students become so interested in the subject after an interview that they develop a lifelong interest in the topic, apply for summer internships, or eventually end up with a part-time job in the field. Take this opportunity to encourage such students to expand their interviews for authentic audiences, such as submitting their piece for local or school newspapers or by creating a blog on the topic.

One middle school ELA teacher had students conduct interviews with faculty members about their favorite books. The students then decided they would interview each other about their favorite books, creating a virtual reading frenzy as students began reading unique books for their interview. Students, on their own, then began posting reviews to Amazon and checking out websites of young adult writers. A few students actually gained a bit of notoriety with their dogged pursuit of interviews from famous authors.

Meredith Edmonds

Seniors Allyson Hart and Meghan Racine listen intently as classmates discuss their inquiry projects in the school library.

5. INDEPENDENT (OR SMALL-GROUP) INQUIRY PROJECT

This activity is at the core of inquiry as it fully engages students in the process. There are countless ways of approaching the project depending upon your topic, discipline, and purpose. Try it, revise it, and discover for yourself how inquiry really does prompt deep learning.

How It Works

There are many ways of organizing inquiry projects depending on the discipline, topic,

A US history teacher used the Library of Congress feature "Former Slaves Tell Their Stories" at memory.loc.gov/ammem/collections/voices/index.html. The almost seven hours of recorded interviews also included full texts of the interviews. Students had to choose one of the interviews and make notes about what else the interviewer could have asked or followed up on. After they read the interview, students then had to read about the interviewee and research him or her to see what else they could find out. Finally, they had to interview someone in their community who had lived there before a major change took place, such as before there was a mall or before the interstate highway came in. Students enhanced their interviews with photos or other artifacts and then made presentations to the city's historical society one evening. The room was packed with members of the society, parents, and the media.

and students. The key is to be flexible and experiment with various ways of facilitating such projects. Following on pages 136–139 are suggestions and tools for getting started.

Why It Works

If you haven't read Daniel Pink's *Drive* (2011), I recommend that you do so or, if you want a quick summary, read an article I wrote based on his ideas titled "The Responsibility Breakthrough" in *Educational Leadership* (Lent, 2010). You'll see that Pink advocates three components necessary for motivation—autonomy, purpose, and mastery—and he provides compelling examples of just how effective these factors can be. Besides employing all three elements of Pink's theory, an independent inquiry project also taps into intellectual risk-taking, allowing students to try on the garments of experts in the disciplines. At the very least, they will understand the struggles that real-world historians, mathematicians, writers, or scientists experience when solving problems or grappling with concepts through research and thinking.

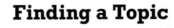

Finding a Topic

Have students create a section in their learning logs to record topics, concepts, questions, or problems related to topics in your discipline that they would like to investigate further. At the end of each grading period or semester, students will look over their list and choose one area of investigation that they will turn into a question to research individually, with a partner, or within a small group. Following are examples of inquiry questions students have researched in various disciplines:

- **Science.** What are the effects on humans of BHPs in plastics that hold food or water?

- **Social Studies.** How are American Indians preserving their culture in the 21st century?

- **Math.** What is an estimate of how much you (or your family) will spend on gas over the next five years based on a certain make and model of car?

- **ELA.** What caused Edgar Allan Poe's fascination with the macabre, based on what we know of his life?

This project could be adapted in many ways. Students may work on the same question, for example, with different topics or texts. In one school, students posted math problems on Edmodo for online conversations to extend learning beyond their peers. In another, students began working together on a project to find out how the lives of the elderly changed when they were unable to live without assistance. The website www.webinquiry .org contains full-blown lessons on a variety of content-area topics such as the following:

- What is El Niño's effect on the weather?

- How can elevation and latitude be used to predict the weather?

- What was the Chinese experience during the construction of the transcontinental railroad?

- How are the works of Paul Laurence Dunbar, Maya Angelou, and Alicia Keys linked?

Getting Started

After students formulate a question, concept, or problem to investigate, they should submit a contract to you for approval, such as the one in Figure 4.5. Each student will meet with you several times over the course of the project, especially if it the project is long term. If students change the focus of their research or inquiry, they should submit a revised contract such as the one in Figure 4.6.

Figure 4.5

Student Plan for Inquiry Project

Name(s):

Date:

Topic to be investigated	
Initial research question	
What information do you plan to collect to answer the question?	
How do you plan to conduct the research (through websites, books, articles, interviews, experiments)?	
What is your proposed timeline for completing the project by the due date?	
How will you present your findings to your group (or the class)? (Example: Prezi, experiment, demonstration, video, text)	

Figure 4.6

Plan for Revising Inquiry Project

Name(s):

Date:

Has your topic changed since our initial conference? If so, when and why?	
Has your research question changed since our initial conference? If so, what is it now? Why did you change it?	
What evidence, data, or information have you collected that may have influenced the change?	
What more do you need to learn to complete the project?	
How do you plan to find what you need?	
How are you managing your time to ensure that your project is complete by the deadline?	
Has your method of presentation to your group of the class changed? If so, how will you present your findings?	

Available for download at http://resources.corwin.com/lentDL

Logistics

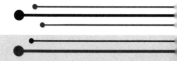

You may want to provide several days in class for students to research or you may require that most of the work be done outside of class with a day or more for in-class feedback from you and the students. Teacher feedback will come in the form of conferences; student feedback could involve having one student explain his progress to a partner with the partner asking questions. Help students pace themselves and pay attention to all aspects of the project: researching, synthesizing what they have learned, and creating a format for presentation. Remember that the goal is the inquiry itself since students learn by engaging in the process.

Learning About Learning

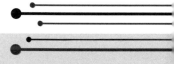

Self-reflection is an important aspect of all inquiry so that students come to know their own strengths and challenges for future endeavors, whether in school, college, or in their careers. Talk with students about metacognition, or learning about learning. A good way to help students become aware of this aspect of learning is to have them keep an inquiry journal, which is a place for student reflections regarding the process and the content. They should use the journal as experts do in the real world to make notes of their learning and reflect on what that learning means. Point out that an inquiry log is somewhat different from a journal or notebook. The log is used to help students keep track of the process by making specific notes about what they've done and where they intend to go with their research, a sort of map of their inquiry. It might be helpful to have students ask experts in the field how they keep track of projects because the process would certainly look different for engineers, writers, historians, or scientists.

Heather Lattimer (2014) gets it right when she says in *Real-World Literacies: Disciplinary Teaching in the High School Classroom*, "The sense of responsibility, reflectiveness and pride of ownership is necessary for life outside of high school, where grades are not assigned, standardized tests don't determine job or career prospects, and success is determined by a willingness to work hard, take ownership, and engage as a learner, always seeking to improve" (p. 16). Teaching students how to create, research, plan, and carry out projects that are relevant to them and important to society is at the heart of education.

Extend and Adapt

At Fern Creek Traditional High School in Louisville, Kentucky, a school I explore in more depth in Chapter 6, students enrolled in a program cotaught by a social studies and English teacher complete what is termed a *Curiosity + Challenge* project. The equation means that the project begins with a student's curiosity and a challenge is added. Students announce and share the topics of their projects before winter break to encourage interest and commitment. Then, each student chooses two classmates who will check in on them over the break. Brent Peters, English teacher, says, "In this way, we see not only collaboration happen over the winter break, but also the formation of new friendships and the building of a community that supports each other outside of class." Interestingly, the teachers also engage in a Curiosity + Challenge project themselves, "modeling our own desire to challenge ourselves and the enthusiasm (and fear) associated with taking on a meaningful challenge."

Fifteen-year-old Pearly Mortley, an avowed carnivore, wanted to know what it was like to be a vegetarian. "What's the appeal?" she asked. "But more than that, could I really become a vegetarian, even for two weeks?" That was the challenge part of her project. She admitted that her family was shocked when she told them of her plans, but she did, indeed, eat no meat for two weeks and ended up blogging about her experience as well as producing a series of video blogs called a vlog.

Christina Logsdon, another Fern Creek student, decided to satisfy her curiosity about the challenges of being a neonatal nurse by shadowing one for two hours and writing about her experiences.

Faruk Ramic wanted to know how animation could be made more challenging so he created software for gaming. First, he made two sketchbooks of original drawings and texts to form a big picture idea for his video game concept. Once he had a big idea, he then set out to create a part of his game using online templates and his own knowledge

Teaching students how to create, research, plan, and carry out projects that are relevant to them and important to society is at the heart of education.

Brent Peters and Joe Franzen

Students at Fern Creek Traditional High School engage in a class "share out."

of graphic design. Faruk is also taking a graphic design class, so the opportunity to explore an idea like this allowed him to combine and stretch his knowledge.

Since inquiry is an inherent part of everyday learning at Fern Creek High, students simply adapted the mindset they use in class to embark on their Curiosity + Challenge projects. Their inquiry is sustained as students present their project over the course of a school year. Brent explains, "We post our progress in our class discussion board and facilitate in-class 'Share outs.' Some students bring in their projects and want to present right away so we schedule that time. Or they complete 'check-ins' over the course of the school year. Some of these projects are ongoing and move students into volunteering over the summer at the Louisville Zoo, at an animal shelter, or Home of the Innocents (youth shelter), for example."

Inquiry is all about returning to the child within all of us who asks questions as a way of coming to know the world into which they have been thrown. Many students have also been thrown into a discipline about which they know very little—and too many times they are prohibited from engaging in the time-consuming, often untidy, process of inquiry.

Teaching our students how to satisfy their curiosity in each discipline may turn out to be the tipping point from an obsolete model of transmission for testing to the information age's paradigm of learning in order to both understand *and* do.

Suggestions for Further Reading

Engaging Readers and Writers With Inquiry: Promoting Deep Understandings in the Language Arts and the Content Areas by Jeffrey Wilhelm, 2008.

Essential Questions: Opening Doors to Student Understanding by Jay McTighe and Grant Wiggins, 2013.

Making Number Talks Matter: Developing Mathematical Practices and Deepening Understanding by Cathy Humphreys and Ruth Parker, 2015.

Powerful Learning: What We Know About Teaching for Understanding by Linda Darling-Hammond et al., 2008.

Succeeding With Inquiry in Science and Math Classrooms by Jeff C. Marshall, 2013.

Uncovering Student Thinking in Mathematics: Grades 6–30: 30 Formative Assessment Probes for the Secondary Classroom by Cheryl M. Rose and Carolyn B. Arline, 2009.

What's the Big Idea? Question-Driven Units to Motivate Reading, Writing, and Thinking by Jim Burke, 2010.

"Why Won't You Just Tell Us the Answer?" Teaching Historical Thinking in Grades 7–12 by Bruce Lesh, 2011.

Making it Relevant

1. Think about an inquiry project you had to do in school or college. Reflect on your attitude toward the project, what you learned, and how the experience may have differed from some of your other school experiences.

2. Target a specific topic in your curriculum that you often teach through transmission. Specifically, how could you engage students in inquiry so they develop a deeper understanding of the content?

3. If you could take a sabbatical and do research on any topic, what would that be? Why do you want to learn about the topic? How could you transfer the desire you have to learn more about a topic to your students?

Notes:

COLLABORATIVE LEARNING

High school teachers Colleen Zenner, Justin Stroh, and Lauren Pennock put their heads together and came up with a project for their Earth science students that used both inquiry and collaboration, the best of all learning practices. The project involved having students construct a seismic-safe structure while staying within a preset budget. Funds for the project came from a grant the teachers had written the previous year that also allowed them to purchase an electronic seismic simulator that shakes student-built structures by simulating the P, S, and L waves of an earthquake.

In groups of three or four, students assumed "real-world" roles: project leader, treasurer, and architect. They then created a company name and logo design before beginning the actual work of researching the structure of a tall building and creating a blueprint design with color-key coding and dimensions for their structure. Students built the models using balsa wood, wood planks (coffee stirrers), popsicle sticks, and any other necessary materials as long as they did not go over budget and followed the guidelines (two stories, no taller than 25 cm, for example).

Just like experts in the field, students used an accounting log to create a budget for their project. They learned how to complete purchase orders and write checks for building supplies, which were submitted as orders to the "warehouse" to be filled. Students also discovered that they could buy insurance to cover replacement parts due to possible damage prior to the testing date.

Each student had to individually prepare a write-up of the project, but they presented the finished structure as a group, explaining areas of weakness and strength. Then, it was time for the groups to test their buildings on the electronic earthquake machine. Because many of the groups' structures passed the earthquake test, it came down to who could construct it for the lowest cost. Colleen said, "Groups who were not successful with the actual structure provided a valuable forum for class discussion as to why the structure did not stay intact. Students discussed what improvement could be implemented next time to ensure success. So the focus was not on *their* failure but a structural design failure."

These teachers knew that real assessment of learning has less to do with how many buildings passed the test and more to do with students' ability to work well together and deeply understand the principles not only of earthquakes but also of buildings that can withstand them. That's why they had students complete an online reflection about what they learned academically as

Colleen Zenner

Construction begins on a seismic-safe structure.

well as what they learned about the dynamics of working together. Colleen pointed out that what students *did not* say was as important as any reflection they may have written. "I don't think I heard one student ask 'Why are we doing this?' 'When am I ever going to need to know this?' or amazingly, 'Is this going to be on the test?'" Since this activity mirrors the procedures of architectural engineers as they determine the structural integrity of buildings prior to construction, we see an important principle of disciplinary literacy in the classroom—doing the work of scientists in place of reading about it.

I'm sure that these same teachers discussed with their classes the April 28, 2015, earthquake in Nepal that killed thousands of people and caused buildings to virtually crumble into rubble. Their students, no doubt, will have a much greater understanding of the events that occurred there than those who simply studied a unit titled "What is an earthquake?" from a science textbook.

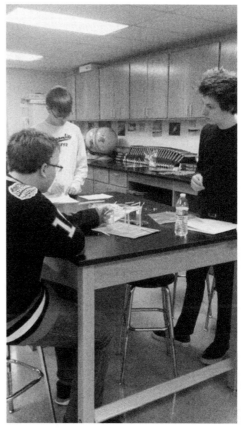

Students in earth science work together to create a seismic-safe structure.

The Power of Collaboration

When teachers work with each other, they often find it easier to incorporate collaborative learning into their instruction, perhaps because they have experienced the advantages of socially constructed work themselves.

In fact, as teachers collaborate, the intellectual stimulation and personal engagement becomes almost addictive, leading them to want their students to experience the same positive aspects of learning together.

If you're not yet convinced of the power of collaboration (both for teachers and for students), and its advantages are many, I recommend a book titled *Deeper Learning: How Eight Innovative Public Schools Are Transforming Education in the Twenty-First Century* (Martinez & McGrath, 2014). Besides highlighting schools that have made the transition, the authors also offer a "Blueprint for Deeper Learning." Of the four aspects necessary for deeper learning, one is collaborative learning communities. They say,

> Collaborating well is an increasingly necessary skill in our modern world. Teaching it is no simple exercise and requires a range of efforts, including inspiring students to care about each other's success, establishing norms for constructive feedback, stimulating those who seem less motivated, and knowing when and how to intervene—and when and how to step aside and allow students to find their way. (p. 50)

The idea seems to be catching on. In California, for example, school districts are increasingly turning to project-based learning as a way to meet Common Core State Standards (Ellison & Freedberg, 2015). Teacher Sara Siebert puts her finger on why collaborative learning works: "They [students] don't realize how hard they are working. They are collaborating with peers. They are able to be creative. They are disagreeing along the way, but from those disagreements comes better work. These are all skills they will be able to use throughout life" (Ellison & Freedberg, 2015, p. 2).

Collaborative Learning by Any Other Name

Collaborative learning has many faces: partner sharing, group discussions, literature or inquiry circles, book clubs, Socratic Seminars, problem- or project-based learning, as well as disciplinary and interdisciplinary projects (within and outside of school). What all of these practices have in common is the negotiation and construction of meaning through communication and clarification of ideas and actions within a respectful and interdependent community. It's more than just grouping students to fill out a worksheet or jigsaw a reading assignment.

This approach involves learning how to use the language of the discipline, listen carefully to another perspective, hold on to thinking, question the status quo, and *participate* in the activities of a discipline to construct meaning. Maybe the very reason that collaboration is so valuable is that it forces its participants to learn and practice so many important skills.

When I ask teachers if it's worth the effort to coordinate such learning, they often admit that it can be challenging to fit all the pieces together, but I have yet to hear a teacher say he or she wants to go back to the transmission model of teaching once they've ventured into collaborative learning. As you can see from the many examples I provide from real teachers in this and other chapters, deep learning and satisfying teaching hinge on student engagement through inquiry and collaboration.

Collaborative learning is more than just grouping students to fill out a worksheet or jigsaw a reading assignment. It is the negotiation and construction of meaning.

Vocabulary: The Tool of Disciplinary Talk

Before we go further, however, I must address an essential component of collaborative learning, discipline-specific language, often referred to as *academic vocabulary*. As you know, the teaching of vocabulary has been the subject of countless professional books, articles, and inservice sessions, and there are many strategies, programs, and scripts for vocabulary instruction. In the end, however, vocabulary learning must be individualized and discipline specific.

The simple word *conclusion*, for example, begins to look less simple when viewed across content areas. A conclusion in science is precise and based on data, unlike a conclusion to a short story or novel, which can be up for interpretation or evaluation. A conclusion in history is often based on evidence, but not necessarily based on quantifiable data as in math or science; rather, it may be grounded in accounts and other primary documents. The very definition of conclusion in math involves a conceptual understanding of a rather complicated definition: A mathematical conclusion is a statement arrived at by applying a set of logical rules known as syllogisms to a set of premises. Furthermore, the process of drawing conclusions from premises and syllogisms is called *deduction*.

So, engaging in "talk" within disciplines, a key skill for collaboration, means that students should become aware of how language works in that content area by developing rich understandings of key concepts. Repetition and integration of important vocabulary are essential practices for conceptual word study within content areas because, after all, students must have the tools to engage in collaborative discussion.

Laura Robb (2014) makes the point in her book *Vocabulary IS Comprehension: Getting to the Root of Text Complexity* that vocabulary study is rarely given sufficient time in instruction. I couldn't agree more. Students must be able to understand conceptually dense words in order to comprehend a text, and they also must be able to use such words appropriately when engaged in collaborative learning.

Collaborative Vocabulary Learning Within the Disciplines

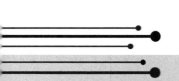

- Give students plenty of opportunities to use new vocabulary in relevant settings.

- Encourage varied ways of coming to know words, such as through drawings, skits, songs, cartoons, stories, and personal connections.

- Don't overload kids with too many words per unit/topic/week. It is better for students to have conceptual understandings of a few key terms than a whole list of superficial definitions.

- Use performance assessments (e.g., demonstrations, projects, speeches, constructions, simulations) where students work together to "show" the meanings of concepts rather than assessing vocabulary through pen and paper tests.

- Allow students to collaborate on graphic organizers such as a Frayer Chart to explore the meanings of words and then share, perhaps through a gallery walk.

- Allow teams of students to take turns creating word walls for specific units. Encourage them to display meanings of words in various ways.

- Teach words within the context of students' reading and provide plenty of opportunities for students to talk with their peers about word meanings as they read.

- Have students keep their own vocabulary lists in their learning logs based on their reading or words that they particularly have difficulty remembering or understanding. Periodically, ask them to share new word entries with their learning partner.

Spotlight on Foreign Language

In foreign language classes, vocabulary is extremely important, as is academic talk—and both are much more difficult than in regular classes since students are often speaking in a foreign language. Spanish teacher Marta Constenla thought it was important for her students to learn these skills, so she engaged them in a collaborative project by asking them to individually answer the following questions:

- How does your culture influence your own identity?

- How does a person's identity develop through time?

- How do language and culture influence someone's identity?

- How is someone's identity portrayed depending on a specific situation?

She then had students share their responses with three classmates before engaging them in a whole-class discussion. After the discussion, Marta gave her students an article (in Spanish) about Francisco Nicolas Gomez, a law student who was arrested for forgery, fraud, and identity theft. She asked students to come together in small groups to discuss the article and choose vocabulary words from their reading to present to the class. Students then watched a short video about Francisco from a Spanish TV station, where they discovered that he was so popular in Spain that a night talk show created a rap song for him.

Students then reunited with their original partner and were told to research two other identity forgers like Nicolas. She provided them with the following guidelines:

- Find one person from the Hispanic community and one from the world at large who has forged his or her identity.

- Write bios in Spanish of both subjects and include a picture.

- Include a list of new Spanish words that you used in your bios. Define the words in a "student-friendly" way.

- Compare and contrast the lives of both.

- Explain to the class, in Spanish, why these people had the need to alter their identities as well as any consequences and benefits of their actions.

- Be prepared to answer questions from your classmates.

Marta said the activity not only helped students learn Spanish vocabulary but it also built community and a sense of camaraderie in her class.

Shifts for Implementing Collaborative Learning Within the Disciplines

An inquiry-based approach to teaching, as described in Chapter 4, requires significant shifts similar to those necessary for implementing collaborative practices within the disciplines. Take a look at the shifts in the shaded box on the next page and consider the adjustments you might need to make in order to incorporate more collaborative practices within your classes.

While collaborative learning may appear similar in all content areas—I picture students gathered in groups actively participating in a task—there are significant differences in how and what they are learning depending upon the discipline.

Brent Peters and Joe Franzen

Students are grouped for collaborative learning in Brent Peters' ELA class.

Collaboration Within Science

As we saw in Chapter 4, collaboration in science almost always begins with a question. Students then work together to observe, collect, record, and analyze pertinent information to

Shifts for Implementing Collaboration Within the Disciplines

- Utilize think-pair-share or some adaptation of this simple practice to get kids accustomed to talking to each other about your content. Don't worry if all students aren't on task at first. The more opportunities they have for quick talks or a brief "turn and talk" in some form, the more they will learn to respond maturely to your prompt.

- Reduce whole-class instruction to shorter mini-lessons and move the actual "work," including discussions, into small groups. Instead of always explaining concepts, principles, or new information to students, for example, give them opportunities to work together to construct explanations.

- Don't panic if you discover that your students have misconceptions while engaged in collaborative learning. The talk they engage in will help you know what misinformation to correct as they articulate their thinking about an essential idea. It is especially important in math and science to understand students' faulty thinking.

- Think of collaboration as the socialization of intelligence and work toward establishing an environment where students feel safe expressing their thoughts, opinions, questions, and confusions—and such risk-taking often occurs first in a small group. Try to relinquish some control, moving from the traditional teacher who imparts information into the role of a facilitator who elicits it.

- Create tasks that support collaborative work, for example, from individual writing assignments to group creation of digital stories (see pages 156–157).

support or disprove a hypothesis. Lab spaces were designed for just such activities, and it is often this type of collaboration that comes to mind when we envision group work in science.

Labs are only the beginning of scientific collaboration, however, and it is worth noting that many science classrooms still rely heavily on lecture and textbooks, with labs as an add-on rather than as a major bridge to learning. The important work in science results from *cognitive wrestling*, a term that describes students engaged in the complexities of deep thinking used at the Institute for Learning at the University of Pittsburgh.

Students learn how to think scientifically by looking for patterns, exceptions, and relationships. Small groups analyzing weather patterns in various parts of the world, for example, might each communicate their findings to the rest of the class and then return to their home group to discuss new understandings or refine their explanations.

What behaviors are exhibited in science classrooms where collaboration is the norm rather than the exception? See the shaded box below.

A Picture of Collaboration in Science

In science classes where collaboration is evident, you may find students

- Working together on formulating and conducting an experiment with various students taking different roles but all involved in the procedure

- Collecting data from various sources

- Evaluating data and determining which is most useful for supporting a hypothesis or solving a problem

- Discussing ideas and perspectives, especially when more evidence is needed to form a conclusion

- Determining how to present findings or explanations

- Creating projects to demonstrate or test hypotheses

- Debating alternate explanations

- Providing feedback to each other

- Investigating real-world issues and using the tools of the discipline to make hypotheses or generate solutions

While it's true that some of these activities can be done individually, the formation of a scientific community where students discuss their ideas and hold each other accountable for their findings and reasoning moves students toward the actual work of science.

Collaboration Within Math

A math class may not be the first place that comes to mind when you think of collaboration, but good math teachers from elementary to high school are enjoying the advantages in having students work together to solve problems and develop conceptual understandings. In the past, students listened to instruction, practiced doing problems in the remaining time before class was dismissed, completed homework (where they practiced even more problems), and returned the next day to have their homework checked. Teaching the underlying principles of math became the primary focus of instruction rather than fostering mathematical understandings.

In today's math classroom, while practice is still important, the emphasis has shifted from only teaching the principles of math to helping students develop deeper mathematical knowledge—and such instruction often includes collaboration.

A Picture of Collaboration in Math

Prompts such as the following spark math discussion and collaboration:

- What does the problem say? What does the problem mean? How would the answer be different if ____ in the problem were changed to ____?

- In what other ways could this problem be solved?

- How does the approach for solving an open-ended math problem differ from that of solving a closed problem?

- What patterns do you see in the three problems assigned to your group?

- How would you create a chart or other visual to demonstrate your thinking about the problem?

- How would the mathematical understanding needed to solve this problem be used in real-world situations?

- How is this problem different from or similar to others we've solved in class?

- Work with your group to explain why . . .

(Continued)

(Continued)

- Show the rest of the class what this concept looks like, perhaps through a graphic, chart, or model.
- Convince another group that your approach to this problem is best.

Collaboration in math means that students have opportunities to hear and consider the thinking of their peers as they develop skills necessary for transferring their learning to other mathematical areas.

Spotlight on Math

Contributed by Meg Gaier Knapik,
middle school math teacher and coauthor
of the 2014 book *Literacy Lessons for
a Digital World: Using Blogs, Wikis, Podcasts,
and More to Meet the Demands of the Common Core*

In my math classroom, collaboration is of paramount importance. In fact, some of the most exciting and productive math activities have been collaborative projects.

With partners, my students wrote math picture books together to create real-life math stories related to the concepts of percentages. Many of the stories focused on shopping (sales tax, percent discount) and calculating tips at a restaurant. Students worked in pairs to write a draft of the story. Then, using a storyboard template the students determined the layout for the iBook, including what words, images, and math problem-solving strategy would be shown on each page. Most students used the Book Creator app on their iPads to publish iBooks, while a few opted to create tangible picture books. The results were fabulous!

Students posted their iBooks to our online learning management system (Schoology), and the tangible books were added to our class library. The students loved reading each other's percentage picture books! Not only were they able to enjoy the entertaining story lines, but they also were able to read a variety of explanations for finding the percentage of a number and using the skill in real life.

My students also love to work in small groups to produce math video tutorials. The students have done in this in a variety of ways. Some students enjoy using the iPad app Explain Everything to create screen cast videos of their problem-solving process, while others prefer to use the video filming capability of the iPad and use iMovie to edit (if necessary). Most recently, my students created video tutorials to explain how to simplify algebraic expressions. The students worked in groups of three or four to decide

Meg's middle school students collaborate on their math tutorials.

on a way to make their thinking visible. Some students used algebra tiles, some drew bar models, and others used a system of underlining and boxing like terms. They also had to brainstorm important math vocabulary to use in their video explanations. Finally, after the planning process was complete the students filmed their math video tutorials with their group members. As a class, we generally view two or three videos together to compare and contrast the strategies and explanations.

The most exciting part for my students is finding out if their video makes it onto our class YouTube channel! Only the videos that correctly use math vocabulary to support and explain their problem-solving process are featured on our channel. These quality videos become wonderful resources for all my students—and anyone else who searches these topics on YouTube.

Collaboration Within History and Social Studies

If math classes are not traditionally the places we would find collaboration, social studies classes may be the best fit. There is not much sadder than to see students come to know history only through what they read in textbooks. History is as alive as any subject could possibly be, and the discipline is supported, clarified, and expanded through talking and listening. Anyone who doubts this has not watched Ken Burns' *The Roosevelts*, for example, and discussed what they learned with another viewer.

A Picture of Collaboration in History and Social Studies

Students might collaborate in social studies classes by doing the following:

- Discuss the context of an event by researching the time period and sharing what they've found with other groups.
- Pull together threads of a historical event through existing texts and convince other groups of the accuracy of their viewpoint.
- Situate themselves in history by exploring how certain groups or cultures played a role, especially if that role is omitted from the textbook.
- Debate interpretations, perspectives, or ethics of historical or current events.
- Role-play events, speeches, or conflicts in history with an awareness of differing viewpoints.
- Compare a current event to a similar one or to a historical corollary.
- Compare, contrast, and analyze different accounts of the same event by using a graphic organizer or other tool to guide the discussion.
- Talk through a difficult text by reading chunks individually and then "saying something" to the group as discussion starters.
- Simulate trials of famous court scenes.
- Analyze visual primary documents and share responses.

- Create cartoons, websites, blogs, newspapers, or other documents based on research.
- Create group projects to share with younger students.
- Simulate periods in history through music, costumes, and speeches.
- Examine social justice issues and take appropriate action (i.e., letters, forums, interviews).

There are endless ways of creating collaborative activities in this discipline, as all good social studies teachers know. The National Council for the Social Studies offers excellent lessons for all courses, most of which emphasize collaborative learning at www.socialstudies.org/teacherslibrary. To access the lessons, readers must be members of the council, but membership is a worthy investment.

History is under the umbrella of *social* studies for a reason; students must engage in the social intellectualization necessary to fulfill the promise of such a fascinating subject.

Collaboration Within ELA

Most students have been fortunate enough to have had an English teacher who can effectively guide a class discussion in ways that help them develop understandings of rich concepts embedded in literature and nonfiction. While whole-class discussions are beneficial in some cases, relying *only* on this approach can be problematic. It misses the mark, for instance, with students who sit quietly in class, perhaps listening, but not actively participating or saying as little as possible even when asked a specific question—and many students drift off when the discussion doesn't directly involve them.

All students need the opportunity to learn how to participate in the authentic give-and-take of a dialogue where they engage in the risks necessary for growth.

All students need the opportunity to learn how to participate in the authentic give-and-take of a dialogue where they engage in the risks necessary for growth.

Small-group collaboration requires that *all* students interact with the text and with each other. It is such talk that allows students to challenge others' interpretations and clarify their own understandings as they learn how to become a part of a literate academic community.

Some of the most joyful learning I have ever witnessed has occurred in ELA classes where students passionately discuss text, especially challenging text, in small groups. When asked what they learned after working with peers, students in a Massachusetts middle school seemed surprised that they were able to read and understand such complex text. They said they completed tasks they would not have even attempted on their own and felt pride in their group's presentation.

A Picture of Collaboration in ELA

Working with others in an ELA class means students have opportunities to

- Develop skills necessary for oral interpretations of texts
- Defend their responses to texts
- Collaborate when finding textual evidence to support opinions and interpretations
- Share strategies for comprehension or have opportunities to approach texts in ways suggested by others
- Reflect on and respond to peers' comments and questions
- Ask questions in a safe environment and learn how to appropriately challenge others' ideas
- Share ideas in prewriting activities
- Improve writing through peer and small-group feedback and revision
- Develop demonstrations of learning through teamwork
- Struggle with complex ideas, themes, and questions through speaking and listening
- Engage in literature circles, seminars, and other structured small-group formats
- Create group performances
- Use the social practices of technology to enhance reading, writing, and thinking

High school English teachers Jolene Heinemann and Stephanie Weiss found that having their students collaborate with others to rehearse, peer-review, and perform together *Romeo and Juliet* in the school's theater created an authentic experience for the students. "The performances also led to a closer reading and better understanding of the play than they had in the past as demonstrated by their literary analysis and written responses at the end of the unit," Jolene said. ELA teachers are fortunate to have a curriculum that lends itself to such rich social practices.

Questions (and Answers) About Collaboration Within the Disciplines

I've never had very much luck with collaborative grouping unless I spend a lot of time structuring the learning. By the time I finish with such extensive planning, I may as well just plan and execute the lesson myself. Am I missing something?

Sometimes collaborative learning does take more time initially, but the benefits of teaching kids how to work in teams and apply knowledge from classroom lessons as they develop independence can be significant. Many studies have concluded that students working in groups learn more and do better on assessments than individuals learning on their own (Darling-Hammond et al., 2008). What's more, employers have made it clear that they want employees who can communicate, collaborate, and think critically and creatively while displaying ingenuity, innovation, and risk-taking. These skills and characteristics don't just appear when someone has a diploma in hand. They develop when students learn to construct meaning and address problems with others on a regular basis. So, the first part of the answer to this question is that the work it takes to implement collaborative learning is simply worth it.

Many studies have concluded that students working in groups learn more and do better on assessments than individuals learning on their own.

By way of advice, I would add that maybe you're trying to structure too much. The more kids *do,* the more they learn. Often, the same can be said about talk. When the teacher is doing all of the talking, students may be passively listening or not listening at all. Try shifting some of the preparation to your students and allow them to learn leadership and organizational skills as they take on some of the logistical burdens.

Create data teams, for example, in science or document finders in history. Have students come up with additional questions for discussion or create roles for members in the groups. Older students are more than capable of finding supplemental texts related to topics for small-group reading, and this task also helps them learn how to identify credible sources. Give students ownership of a project, especially one where they can experience the results, such as a service-learning project, and then be prepared to move out of the way because once students own a project, they often go far beyond the requirements of the assignment.

Remember, too, that collaborative learning takes time to evolve, so proceed with patience. Kids don't come to school knowing how to move from social to academic talk, so setting norms and scaffolding this challenging but essential skill is mandatory for success. In Harvey Daniels and Nancy Steinke's 2014 book *Teaching the Social Skills of Academic Interaction, Grades 4–12: Step-by-Step Lessons for Respect, Responsibility, and Results*, they discuss how teachers can explicitly teach such skills and provide engaging lessons for creating a culture of respectful communication within classrooms.

In any case, resist the urge to return to the obsolete "sage on stage" paradigm. If the first collaborative learning experience seems, as a middle school social studies teacher put it, "over the top chaotic," don't give up. Try to pinpoint the challenges and address them one at a time. Also, give the groups time to settle into the discussion or project, and don't cut it off before they have time to experience the satisfaction of real dialogue, a major component of *doing* within the discipline.

Kids know how to talk, that's for sure, but I'm not convinced such talk really increases learning. Often their talk is superficial or off task. How can I ensure that they are really learning through collaboration?

It's true that not all talk, even talk that is directed by a targeted assignment, is productive. "Accountable Talk," a principle developed by Sarah Michaels, Mary Catherine O'Connor, Megan Williams Hall, and Lauren Resnick (2002), suggests that students must be accountable to three separate entities when they engage in academic discussion: to their learning community, to knowledge itself, and to their own rigorous thinking.

Such responsible interaction responds to and furthers the thinking of others in the group. Furthermore, students who become productive members of an intellectual community learn important skills for career or college, such as how to ask for clarification or explanation, challenge misconceptions, and interpret each other's statements—but we must give them opportunities to practice and hone such skills.

Help students understand how to engage in academic talk by working with them to establish norms for productive discussions and post the agreed-upon norms on the wall. See Figure 5.1 for sample group norms.

Figure 5.1

Sample Norms for Group Discussion

Sample norms for group discussion may include the following:

- Make sure everyone understands the purpose of the discussion.
- Listen actively and openly to what others have to say, take notes and then respond to or develop their points.
- Don't talk over each other. Wait your turn or indicate to the facilitator that you have something to say.
- When you want to challenge someone's thinking, have a reason or evidence for your objection. Always remain respectful and keep comments academic, not personal.
- Make sure your statements are accurate and credible. How do you know what you are saying is true?
- Rephrase for the purpose of clarity if you are unsure about a comment someone has made.
- Invite contributions from everyone, especially those who don't often speak up.

Because talk in math may look different from talk in other disciplines, it helps to generate norms specific to that content area. A good example of accountable-talk norms in math can be found at math.utep.edu/Faculty/duval/class/random/mathaccttalk.html.

General tips from a variety of teachers who have turned their classes into models of collaborative learning are listed in Figure 5.2.

Figure 5.2

Tips for Incorporating Collaborative Learning

- Show students what good conversations look like by facilitating whole-class discussions and pointing out when the discussion is going especially well—and why. Emphasize how to rephrase a student's comment for clarity, challenge a student's thinking with respect, or press for additional information if a comment is sketchy, and encourage everyone to participate. Once students understand what productive talk looks like, you can expect them to begin using it in peer discussions.

- Relevance and autonomy sustain all learning. Groups formed for the purpose of answering questions on a worksheet, for example, encourage off-task behavior and an attitude of "let's get finished with this" instead of deepening learning through intrinsic motivation.

- Collaborative tasks should be sufficiently challenging to elicit engagement and the use of higher-order skills but not so challenging that students drift into boredom or frustration. This may require differentiation of text or assignments.

- Actively work the room, going from group to group to support and facilitate students' collaboration instead of focusing on crowd control. This is the best time to model the fine art of talk by joining in the conversation if appropriate, affirming students' contributions through positive comments or by gently moving the conversation back on target. The goal is for students to be so immersed in their discussion that they hardly notice you're there, not suddenly returning to the task when they see the teacher approaching.

- Some students get distracted by the noise in the room during group work. Keeping groups at three to four helps with the noise and minimizes distractions. The teacher who offered this suggestion said she had one group that worked very productively under a table, for example.

- If you have difficulty with classroom management of small groups, observe another teacher who has an efficient system for small-group work. There are many different ways of grouping students as well as instructional routines for managing groups. Try different methods and don't become discouraged if it takes a while to make this shift.

- Have something for students to do, such as reading, working on an ongoing project, or completing items in their portfolio, if their group finishes before other groups.

I've heard that assigning roles for group work sometimes contributes to a task-oriented discussion instead of a deep learning situation. But without roles, one person may do all the work and let others skate. What's the answer?

The criticism of the use of roles comes from teachers who find that students with a specified role, vocabulary finder, for example, may finish their part, dust off their hands, and be satisfied that they've completed the "work" assigned to them. Individuating a task in such a way is clearly counterproductive to collaboration and interactive communal learning experiences. Especially at first, however, roles may be necessary for students to engage in the often challenging work of peer collaboration. For example, it's almost always helpful to have a facilitator who is responsible for keeping the discussion moving, making sure everyone's voice is heard, and bringing rabbit trails back to the main path. Be sure and rotate this role so students can each experience a leadership position. Other possible roles for disciplinary discussions follow.

- **Researcher:** One who has access to a device and can quickly research an unknown term, concept, event, fact, formula, or background information

- **Recorder:** One who takes notes during the discussion and makes the notes available to others (or the teacher) after the meeting

- **Presenter:** One in charge of making findings available to the class

You might consider a summarizer, fact checker, timekeeper, discussion tracker (one who keeps tracks of the flow of conversation, especially in seminars) or as one teacher liked to assign, a terminator, the person responsible for making sure side conversations and other inappropriate behaviors are eliminated.

Students present their collaborative analysis of the theme of a short story.

At Fern Creek Traditional High School in Louisville, Kentucky, (see Chapter 6) where work more often than not is within small groups, I didn't see even one student off task or not contributing. Pearly Mortley, a sophomore in Brent's English class, said she stayed on task when working in a group, even when her teacher wasn't around because "he trusts us and respects us." Furthermore, the work Brent's students are doing is also for an audience of their peers, so they take pride in their accomplishments and want to contribute for a purpose other than simply for a grade.

Student discussions provide valuable opportunities for monitoring learning rather than evaluating learning, an important distinction.

Are homogenous or mixed-ability groups best? I don't want to hurt my struggling-learners' self-esteem by placing them with higher-achieving students—or hold back my more advanced students.

The debate continues on this question with the two sides providing evidence that supports their respective position. Not surprising, is it? Earlier research indicated that students of all levels experience higher achievement in heterogeneous groups (Lou et al., 1996), but recently there have been some studies that show that homogenous grouping, especially in math and science, may be more beneficial.

The best answer appears to be mixing it up according to your purpose. For example, if you want to build relationships or background knowledge, say, with English language learners and their experiences in countries outside of the United States, heterogeneous groupings would certainly be best. If you want to challenge your advanced learners, you might create groups based on ability.

Often it is beneficial to allow students to choose their group members, especially at first when they may not feel comfortable with everyone in the class. A social studies teacher in Florida found that the quality of students' work as well as their time on task increased when they were given autonomy in the selection of their group. In the end, the purpose for instruction drives the activity as well as any variations in it and, as always, the teacher who really knows her students also knows the best way to facilitate collaboration.

How do I assess collaborative learning? I really don't need any more parents arguing with me over grades I give for group work.

Unfortunately, assessment is one of the major deterrents teachers cite to collaborative learning, and there's no arguing that it can be rather messy to grade. Instead of trying to make a summative assessment fit the group mold, use this time to practice (and become expert at) formative assessment, which is easy to justify to parents because it unequivocally increases learning (McMillan, 2007). Student discussions provide valuable opportunities for *monitoring* learning rather than *evaluating* learning, an important distinction.

Even in this electronic age, I find that a clipboard is still a useful tool for making notes that can be used for individual feedback as well as for planning whole-class lessons. List student names on one side of the page and use a system of checks or brief notes beside the name to record evidence of behaviors and understandings. A form similar to the one in Figure 5.3 is effective.

You might also interject a student self-reflection tool into the mix. Give students time after daily or weekly collaboration to answer questions that lead to self-regulated behaviors and deeper understandings about themselves as learners.

They can either write in their learning logs based on prompts you provide, or they can use a rubric such as the one in Figure 5.4.

In the Earth science example at the beginning of this chapter, the teachers had students complete a self-reflection survey at the conclusion of the project by answering questions such as "What characteristics of a good team member did you exhibit?" This tool not only helped students better process the experience, but it also guided teachers' revision of the activity for the following year.

If a summative grade is necessary, consider giving two grades; one for the group product or performance and another for the individual contribution. Use your formative assessment and individual conference notes to help evaluate individual learning.

You might also want to try giving a group test where you provide the group a harder test than usual. Students work on the problems or questions together, but every person writes the answer and an explanation of how the answer was derived on his or her own paper. Then, the teacher randomly chooses one of the individual's tests from the group to grade, and everyone receives the same score. All students are then accountable for participating in the assessment. This method is especially helpful for collaborative activities in math.

Students need time after collaborative learning to answer questions that lead to self-regulated behaviors and deeper understandings about themselves as learners.

Figure 5.3

Formative Assessment Tool for Collaborative Learning

Student Name	Uses evidence effectively	Is accountable to the group: Listens and builds on others ideas	Shows understanding of key concepts	Asks questions	Presents reasonable arguments	Interacts with peers in respectful manner

Available for download at http://resources.corwin.com/lentDL

Figure 5.4

Student's Self-Reflection Survey for Collaborative Learning

To what extent did I engage in the discussion or work?	I was unable engage in the discussion or work because . . .	I may have dominated the discussion or tried to take over. Explain.	My contribution to the discussion or work was average for me. Explain.	I was pleased with my contribution to the group because . . .
To what extent was I prepared for today's group work?	I was totally unprepared because . . .	I could have been better prepared in this way:	I was adequately prepared. Explain.	I felt I was very well prepared. Provide an example.
How well did I learn with my group today?	I don't feel I learned much in group work today because . . .	Most of what I learned will not be useful in this class because . . .	I learned at least one important thing today. Explain.	Today's group work was a great learning experience because . . .
When the group ran into a problem or challenge, how well did I contribute to the team effort of solving the problem?	I did not participate in the solution. Explain.	I could have done more to help solve the problem. Explain.	I supported the team by contributing to the solution in this way:	I was instrumental in helping my team solve the problem. Explain.

Available for download at http://resources.corwin.com/lentDL

Spotlight on Science

Caroline Milne, a high school biology teacher, uses the illustrations in a picture book titled *The Skin You Live In* by Michael Tyler (2005) as a collaborative summative assessment by asking students to explain how (or if) the images are realistic biologically. She said using visuals in this way elicits more detailed responses from her students. "When students work together on an assessment such as this, it actually becomes a continuation of their learning. They come away from the activity with a better understanding of the concepts I want them to learn." A sample from one of the groups proves her point.

Everyone is different. Whether that means personality, intellect, hair color, eye color, or even skin color. Skin color can be different because of lots of different components within your skin. First of all is a component called melanin. Melanin is a pigment that changes the color of your skin depending on your genetics or exposure to the sun. This means that people with light skin tones have less melanin in their bodies, while people with darker skin tones have more melanin in their bodies. That means that freckles are small patches of skin with a higher concentration of melanin. Carotene is another factor that affects the color of your skin. Carotene production in the body is elevated when you eat carrots or tomatoes. This means that when you eat foods like carrots or tomatoes, your skin can adopt a shade of orange or yellow tint. Hemoglobin is yet another factor which may affect your skin color. Hemoglobin is a pigment in your body that gives blood its color. When hemoglobin meets oxygen, a bright red color is produced, which causes the red or pink flush in your cheeks when you're embarrassed or warm. Skin is not simple. Melanin, carotene, and hemoglobin are some of the factors that result in your skin tone, the tint of your skin as well the flush your skin might have.

I know building community is important for any type of collaboration, but I have some classes where there's just no synergy—or worse, the kids seem to hate each other. Do you have any tips for those types of situations?

We've all had those classes and remember them well. It's difficult to ensure success with any sort of group work when students act out in ways that seem to sabotage our best efforts. English teacher Brent Peters says one of the most important aspects of collaboration is helping students get to know each other as people. "We must learn to listen to each other in order to humanize the discussion and develop reverence for each other, even if we disagree." Such an approach won't happen all at once, especially if students are not accustomed to being trusted and having their thoughts valued.

A student I talked to recently said that as an introvert, she found it hard to do any type of collaboration unless she knew the other members of the group well. Another student said that he never liked being in groups because the work was so regimented and the tasks so narrow that he felt as though he was just following directions with other people in tow, not really building understanding through dialogue or actions. He went on to say that "real" group work means that the students care about each other and have been given the autonomy to make decisions for themselves. "When we rely on each other to come up with something that is important or meaningful, we really begin working *together* rather than just doing what the teacher tells us to do in a group."

The message from all corners is clear: Effective learning can't take place in an environment devoid of relationships. It is essential to make time for building relationships, perhaps by turning the class into a sort of disciplinary think-talk-do tank where students feel safe enough to express themselves, make mistakes, or take academic risks. Daniels and Steinke (2015) write about having kids from rival gangs work in groups. This passage from their book has stayed with me: "For eight years Smokey and several colleagues ran a high school in Chicago where many kids were affiliated with black and Hispanic gangs. Outside of school, some bad things happened. But inside, we never had a gang incident, and

When we rely on each other to come up with something that is important or meaningful, we really begin working together rather than just doing what the teacher tells us to do in a group.

Figure 5.5

Tips for Building Community

Teachers who are adept at building community

- Allow students to engage in talk often with partners, small groups, and the entire class. Hand raising may not be necessary in discussion-rich classrooms as students learn to wait their turn and listen to others. An eighth-grade teacher taught her students to respond to each other with "I agree," "I disagree," or "I would like to add" in place of raising hands. I expected the discussion to be a bit artificial when she described the protocol, but I saw students genuinely engaged with each other instead of talking only to the teacher and waiting to be called upon to say something.

- Encourage students to take ownership of their talk by modeling respect, even if a student says something inappropriate.

- Create community-building events where students share experiences and come to know each other. One teacher encouraged students to show up for classmates who were playing a sport or acting in a play as a show of support.

  At Fern Creek High School, teachers Brent Peters and Joe Franzen create "class community meals" where students bring in the dishes for the meal and then eat together at one long table. See Chapter 6 for more on this practice. Students say that having meals together makes them feel more like family than classmates.

- Employ "*dis*-orientation" rituals, where students' expectations of passive, rote learning practices are disrupted. At the Science Leadership Academy, for example, students are placed in groups and sent out during orientation week to conduct research in downtown Philadelphia and then work together to creatively present their findings (Martinez & McGrath, 2014, pp. 28–19).

- Schools that utilize older students as mentors develop a culture of inclusivity that diminishes bullying and fosters community building. A middle school math teacher takes time when she passes back students' tests for building academic relationships. "Who got Number 4 right?" she asks and then instructs students who missed that problem to gather around the people who solved it correctly to hear their explanation of the solution.

- Have students participate in a Socratic Seminar (see pages 177–179) at the earliest opportunity. The process is ideal for building community and encouraging respectful communication.

kids treated each other with friendliness and support—because the faculty modeled and taught it. What breaks down hate is knowing people. When we know people as individuals, it gets harder and harder to demonize, discount, or disrespect them" (pp. 35–36). Students must have opportunities to get to know each other through meaningful, collaborative work, such as service-learning projects (see page 181). You'll see the barriers disappear and the enthusiasm for learning increase.

Activities for Collaborative Learning Within the Disciplines

1. STUDENT-LED WHOLE-CLASS DISCUSSION

Reciprocal teaching (Palincsar, 1986) is a collaborative activity used successfully in classrooms for bringing meaning to text through teacher-student dialogue. You can find a good model of the practice at www .ncrel.org/sdrs/areas/issues/students/atrisk/at6lk38.htm. The reason this particular activity is successful is because of the truism that says "The best way to learn something is to teach it to someone else." Teachers learn their lessons well, but often this valuable form of learning is denied to students. The following activity puts students in the teacher's shoes and the advantages are evident.

How It Works

Each student in class leads a 5- to 10-minute whole-class discussion on a topic related to the current unit of study. Students may also work together in teams as they facilitate discussions. At the beginning of a unit, the teacher brainstorms topics or questions with students that will prompt quality discussions. This list might be placed on a chart where students can make additional suggestions.

Students then sign up for one of the topics. For example, if a social studies teacher wants students to explore child labor as it relates to the Industrial Revolution, a list of related topics might include *steam power, cotton gin, Luddites, capitalism,* and *railroads*. Students would choose a topic and sign up for a designated day to lead a discussion on the topic. Instead of doing a traditional report, however, the student will research the topic and formulate questions that she will pose to the class on her assigned day. All questions must contain enough background information to sustain a discussion but not so much that dialogue is curtailed. That means the student must summarize and synthesize content when researching the topic, but such skills may need to be explicitly taught.

Example of Student Discussion Plan

Suppose a student chose to do a discussion on Luddites, something most students may never have even heard of before. The student's plan for facilitating a discussion might look like Figure 5.6. In disciplines such as math, students may facilitate discussions around open-ended questions or problems related to the concept being studied.

Figure 5.6

Student Plan for Facilitating a Discussion on the Topic of Luddites

- Background on Luddites to present to the class:

  o *Luddites were 19th century English artisans, people who created things by hand. They didn't like the new machinery of the Industrial Revolution because things could be made faster and cheaper by machines and they were put out of business. They tried to oppose the Industrial Revolution.*

- Questions to prompt discussion about Luddites:

  o *How could the Luddites stop a movement as large as the Industrial Revolution?*

    - Follow-up question: *Luddites often burned factories or smashed machines. What would you say to Luddites if you could go back in history?*

- How could the Luddites have been integrated into the Industrial Revolution?

- Can you think of any modern-day Luddites?

  - If no one says anything, prompt them by suggesting groups such as the present-day Amish or the Hippies from the 1960s or ask them if they know anyone who rejects the use of certain common technologies such as cell phones.

- Extra questions:

  - *The Luddites make me think of the novel and movie,* The Hunger Games. *The people in the Districts had no power. They just wanted to live a simple life. Can you think of other books where characters were like the Luddites?*

Prior to having students act as facilitators, the teacher will model the role of discussion leader for several days, pointing out behaviors that good facilitators exhibit. A chart such as the one in Figure 5.7 may help students understand the role of a facilitator. You also may have students fill in a blank chart with their thoughts before providing your own tips.

Why It Works

Besides giving students practice in speaking and listening, this activity deepens understanding of content-area topics and provides a real context for research. In addition, it allows students to gain self-efficacy in their abilities to facilitate a discussion which will transfer to small-group work. Students also take this activity seriously, probably because of the autonomy and ownership it offers.

A high school English teacher who uses this practice regularly says that conversations often extend into other classes because students become so engaged in the topic of the discussion. He also notes that students come up with amazingly good questions and suggests having the class jot down in their learning logs good questions asked by the student facilitator which they can then use as a model for their preparing their own questions.

Figure 5.7

Facilitators Versus Control Freaks

Facilitators	Control Freaks
Research the topic and prepare a *brief* opening summary or provide *sufficient* background information to prompt discussion.	Research the topic and prepare a *long* opening summary or provide *too much* background information to prompt discussion.
Prepare open-ended questions.	Prepare questions with only one answer.
Come to the group with a genuine sense of inquiry.	Come to the group acting as though they know more than anyone else about the topic.
Give time for peers to think though questions.	Answer questions themselves if no one quickly responds.
Listen attentively, perhaps taking notes to guide follow-up questions.	Think of what they want to say as peers are talking.
Follow up on comments made by peers through clarifying, rephrasing, or questioning.	Try to provide a better response than peers have given.
Make sure everyone's voice is heard and no one dominates the conversation.	Show favoritism by allowing only a few people to talk.
Correct misperceptions respectfully.	Tell peers they are wrong.

Extend and Adapt

Reading skills also can be supported through student-led discussions. Have the facilitator provide a text or link related to the topic and give students time to read the text in class or assign it for homework, asking them to write a response in their learning logs prior to the discussion. Students are often better able to engage in discussions after expanding their knowledge through reading, a practice especially helpful for struggling readers and English language learners.

2. SEMINARS, WITH OR WITHOUT SOCRATES

The best-known seminar for classroom use is the Socratic Seminar, named for Socrates' method of asking questions to find meaning and valuing the process of inquiry over information. In keeping with our focus on disciplinary literacy, I encourage you to take the ideas for this activity and, ideally within your professional learning community (PLC) or with a colleague, adapt the format to create powerful dialogue based on inquiry, questioning, and speaking and listening.

Unlike a whole-class or small-group discussion, a seminar is more formal in nature and is always based on a text. Students generally read the text individually and then engage in a discussion, using protocols that encourage listening, deliberation, and respect. In addition, students practice thinking critically, articulating their thoughts, and responding thoughtfully to the ideas of others.

How It Works

Choose a text that invites inquiry, something that has some ambiguity, is open-ended, or can be viewed from different perspectives. Short stories or poems can be used for ELA, contrasting documents in social studies, an article about a current issue in science or a text that shows a practical application in math, for example. Provide the text to students, either the day before or at the beginning of the seminar, depending upon the text and your purpose. Ask students to read the text carefully and annotate as they read, either in the margins of a handout, on sticky notes, or with an editing tool on a device. In the case of a poem or short article, it may be helpful to have students number the lines for easier reference during the discussion.

Work with students to generate discussion norms similar to those on page 163 and ask students to hold themselves accountable for the norms they create. While it may be necessary to remind students of certain expectations during the seminar, such as not to talk over each other or to remain respectful, the goal is to create a student-led seminar with participants coming to value the process of dialogue. In most cases, students enjoy this activity and take pride in making it a success.

The teacher acts as facilitator, at least at first, using prepared questions that require a generative answer. She takes students back to the text but also encourages thoughtful responses that help students examine their attitudes, beliefs, and understandings. While it is often difficult to help students master such ambiguous skills, resist correcting them during the seminar, relying instead on follow-up questions to shed light on the issue or solicit other perspectives. If misperceptions persist, use mini-lessons following the seminar to clarify understandings.

Encourage students to talk to each other, calling each other by name, rather than a back-and-forth between teacher and student, and try to assume the role of objective facilitator rather than all-knowing teacher.

After the seminar, ask students to reflect on the experience in their learning logs through questions such as the following:

- What insights did you gain from the discussion?
- In what way(s) were you proud of your contributions to the discussion?
- How might you improve your participation in a future seminar?
- What question(s) would you still like to ask?
- What point would you still like to make?

Casey Cuny (2014), high school English teacher, wrote an article titled "What Is the Value of Life? And Other Socratic Questions" that offers practical advice for setting up a Socratic Seminar. Her endorsement of the activity is compelling: "Students spent two class periods discussing the value of life as explored in the assigned texts. The results were astounding. I watched students search through texts for evidence, discuss the language and structure, and connect the material to their own lives." There aren't many activities that garner such high praise from teachers.

If you want more specifics about Socratic Seminars, along with examples from various disciplines, go to ReadWriteThink at www .readwritethink.org/professional-development/strategy-guides /socratic-seminars-30600.html.

Why It Works

Seminars work because they invite students into the very heart of disciplinary learning—using literacy as a vehicle for understanding. Students read (and reread) challenging text, learn to return to the text, think through the author's meaning, use what they have read to inform their own thoughts, listen and respond to others' ideas, engage in metacognition through speaking and writing, and deepen understanding of content. And equally important, students experience the satisfaction of participating in deep learning within a community of peers that they have come to trust. If I were forced to choose only one activity to use in any discipline, guess which one I would choose? Yep. The seminar, hands down.

Extend and Adapt

Try an interdisciplinary seminar. ELA and history work together beautifully, as do math and science, but I've seen some very successful math/ELA seminars as well as history/science collaborations. All it takes is time to plan with your colleague and a common set of students. Take a look at the Teaching Channel's videos on creating a cross-discipline Socratic seminar at www.teachingchannel.org/videos/team-teach-socratic-seminar-nea.

If you'd like to try an adaptation of the Socratic seminar called the Paideia seminar, I recommend Terry Roberts and Laura Billings' (2011) book *Teaching Critical Thinking: Using Seminars for 21st Century Learners,* or you can drop in on a Paideia seminar by reading a script of students' dialogue as they participate in a thoughtful examination of Emma Lazarus' poem, "The New Colossus" in *Common Core CPR: What About the Adolescents Who Struggle . . . or Just Don't Care?* (Lent & Gilmore, 2013, pp. 135–150).

3. BEYOND THE SCHOOLHOUSE WALLS

Take learning outside of the school and tap into immense advantages for students and often for the community. Science students studying botany, for example, take a field trip to a city park and in small groups map the plants and trees in designated areas of the park, looking specifically for invasive species. When they return to class, they compare notes, identify the species, and come up with a plan for eradicating non-native plants that are taking over other vegetation. They then share their plans with the county's parks and recreation manager. Later in the year, the manager asks students for input when making plans for spring landscaping.

How It Works

In deciding on a project, look for one that will immerse students in the work of your discipline as well as making a meaningful impact on others. The National Youth Leadership Council has many resources for and ideas about community service projects related to all disciplines and grade levels on its website at www.nylc.org/. They also sponsor an annual National Service Learning Conference, an exhilarating immersion in learning and doing. If at all possible, consider taking a team of students to one of their conferences, where they can attend a variety of sessions, network with others, and gain ideas for implementing their own service-learning projects. A special feature of the conference is a daylong session called the World Forum. At the 2015 conference, it was titled Beyond Borders, Beyond Boundaries and focused on tackling global issues through service-learning, a perfect match for social studies, ELA, science, career, or leadership classes. If a conference experience isn't feasible, there are plenty of opportunities in your own backyard. See Figure 5.8 for tips on engaging students in service-learning closer to home.

Why It Works

Fred Newmann and Gary Wehlage (1993) describe standards that were associated with what they termed *authentic pedagogy*. I contend these standards (adapted below) also reflect the benefits of beyond-the-schoolhouse-walls projects:

1. Students engage in higher-order thinking required for solving problems and discovering new understandings and meanings *while doing work within the disciplines.*

Figure 5.8

Tips for Engaging Students in Service-Learning Projects

- Give students parameters for the project and have them brainstorm ideas for service-learning related to your topic of study. If possible, ask leaders in the community to come to your class to talk with students about projects that would be beneficial to nonprofit organizations, such as working with the food pantry on how to increase distribution of healthful food to those in need.

- For this type of project, it usually works best if students choose their group members based on a common interest. Sometimes the entire class will work on one service-learning project, with small groups taking on different tasks.

    An American government class that held a candidates' forum, for example, divided tasks into the following: formulating questions, managing logistics, creating publicity, communicating with candidates, facilitating on-site support.

- Provide a planning form but allow students to modify it to fit the project. See an example in Figure 5.9.

- Give students time during class for both planning and implementation, but students are usually so excited about the project that they spend hours outside of class working to complete it. Teachers' biggest challenge often is containing students' enthusiasm.

- Make sure your assessment includes a self-reflection piece asking students to examine what and how they learned through doing. You may need to make explicit that connection.

2. Students tap into depth of knowledge when they work *within a discipline* to develop complex understandings.

3. Students' connectedness to the world helps them understand the larger social context *of the discipline.*

4. Students engage in high levels of substantive conversation as dialogue builds on each other's ideas while *working within the discipline.*

5. Students experience the social support necessary for achieving work *within the discipline.*

Figure 5.9

Student Planning Form for Service-Learning Project

1. Identify a goal, problem, purpose, or objective for the project.

   - How do you know there is a need?
   - Why is this project important?
   - What impact on the community (or segment of the community) will the project have?

2. What steps will you take to implement the project? Include a timeline of actions.

   - What are you going to do? How are you going to do it?
   - What will you need in order to complete your action?

     o resources
     o information
     o permissions
     o other

3. What possible challenges do you foresee? How do you plan to meet the challenges?

4. How will the tasks be divided among the group or class?

5. How will you share what you have learned?

Available for download at http://resources.corwin.com/lentDL

Projects that extend beyond the classroom help students understand why problem solving, questioning, researching, and communicating intrinsically matter.

Extend and Adapt

As a requirement for graduation, many schools include community service projects, senior projects, or even interdisciplinary grade-level

Middle school students collaborate on a hands-on project utilizing the principles of math.

projects. Often community members are invited to view or evaluate the final product or presentation, sometimes in the form of a museum or fair. In one school, for example, math and science teachers had students create a business plan and work together on a new invention in a sort of *Shark Tank* format where teams presented their ideas to local businessmen. Some of the students have gone on to patent their invention or idea, but the real advantage lies in the hard work and deep learning that students experienced. With not a worksheet in sight, these students proved what they had learned by using disciplinary knowledge to create, construct, and defend.

Perhaps our students' greatest hunger lies in their desire to find meaning through community. If social media has taught us little else, it has made clear the desire of young people to connect with and learn from each other. And, now perhaps more than at any other time in history, students need to learn how to become informed, active, participating members of a democracy where they understand how to frame questions, listen to others, scrutinize evidence, and collaborate to solve problems. We can catch this wave by transforming our disciplines into places where students work together to turn knowledge into action.

Suggestions for **Further Reading**

Common Core CPR: What About the Adolescents Who Struggle . . . or Just Don't Care? by ReLeah Cossett Lent and Barry Gilmore, 2013.

Project-Based Learning: Differentiating Instruction for the 21st Century by William N. Bender, 2012.

Teaching the Social Skills of Academic Interaction, Grades 4–12: Step-by-Step Lessons for Respect, Responsibility, and Results by Harvey Daniels and Nancy Steineke, 2014.

Teach Like Socrates: Guiding Socratic Dialogues and Discussions in the Classroom by Erick Wilberding, 2014.

Setting the Standard for Project-Based Learning: A Proven Approach to Rigorous Classroom Instruction by John Larmer, John Mergendoller, and Suzie Boss, 2015.

Making it Relevant

1. When you collaborate with others in your work, what advantages do you experience?

2. When you collaborate with others in your work, what challenges do you face? Do you think students experience these same challenges? How might you help students overcome them?

3. If you have been reluctant to try collaborative learning, what are your reasons? What one step could you take to increase student collaboration in your classroom?

Notes:

THIS IS DISCIPLINARY LITERACY

The last scene of this book provides a picture of disciplinary literacy in action with examples from an unexpected source, a previously failing high school in a small suburb of Louisville, Kentucky.

Fern Creek Traditional High School (FCTHS) was one of the lowest performing schools in Kentucky just a few short years ago. As one of several options offered by the state for failing schools, the administration and over 50 percent of its staff was replaced. Joe Franzen, social studies teacher, and Brent Peters, English teacher, were two of new staff brought on board by the newly appointed principal in 2010. The job facing them was daunting: Most of the students were considered at risk, and the school's reputation in the community had declined significantly over the years. Many students were choosing to go elsewhere, even with the new staff.

Enter: Food Lit

Part of Fern Creek's success story began when Joe started an after-school cooking club and students flocked to the popular teacher for a chance to engage in something authentic, as opposed to "sitting in desks filling out worksheets" as one student described it. Now, five years later, the "club" has turned into a unique team-teaching initiative taught by Joe and Brent that involves an entire curriculum called "Food Lit," with courses spanning pre-AP English to global issues. The program includes a very active cooking club and garden-environmental club as well as summer garden internships and individual research projects most adults would be hard-pressed to complete. To be sure, the initiative is one piece of FCTHS's larger success story, but the club's foundation began with *community*. As Joe describes, "The initiative pulled in home, tradition, family—and challenged what it means to be a teacher, student, peer, or neighbor. We used questioning and personal narratives to move the group to action, expanding the club into the larger program that exists today."

The initiative pulled in home, tradition, family—and challenged what it means to be a teacher, student, peer, or neighbor.

Literacy Alive

Brent says that he first thought of a food lit class when he was taking a class at Bread Loaf School of English, *Hip Hop as Social Justice Texts*. "The class offered me a new way of seeing that food, like hip hop, was already in the class; it just needed to be talked about and 'read' seriously." That idea expanded into an entire food lit curriculum based on reading, writing, inquiry, and collaboration using food as the source of study, but don't get the impression that this is some sort of program for foodies that hooks kids in by only allowing them to eat in class. The day I visited, for example, students were reading *The Bear* by Anton Chekov in their English class and working in small groups to identify and analyze characterization, symbolism, conflict, theme, irony, and performance aspects of the play.

The students working on the performance component of the lesson had transformed itself into an acting company and even created impromptu labor contracts. They rehearsed the play, staged it, and acted it out in class the next day. The other groups had presented their "teach outs" before the play. As Brent explains, "The idea is that the teach outs will invite students to teach each other, and the activity will also create a greater awareness and initial conversation about what students would see in the production." "Write outs" provided another form of understanding before everyone viewed a very enthusiastic performance of the play. A "share out" followed the performance, with Brent leading students toward new realizations that may have occurred while experiencing the play, those that may not have been evident when reading it.

Since this is, after all, a food lit class, students also brought in theater snacks (muffins, gummy bears, etc.) to share during the play. "One of the invitations to analysis writing is to take some of the big questions and ideas that come from class and extend them. Included in these choices for focused analysis writing is a prompt that asks students to make an analogy about how a character or some aspect of the play is like a gummy bear. In some ways the character Smirnoff toward the end of the play becomes less like the 'Bear' he is accused of being and more like a gummy bear. He even says to Popova at the end of the play (and this is so cool!) that 'my mind has turned to jelly, and my joints have turned to sugar.' So somehow the gummy bears we ate in class the day before are now a way to gain entry into the play and allow students to experience another level of irony that we may not have originally intended," said Brent.

Students also use a reading journal in their classes. As one student describes, "It is a space for you to put your thoughts about your novels. Each week Mr. Peters and Mr. Franzen will have a specific list of things for you to include in your journal that will relate to our class. Beyond that, what you write

Students in Brent Peters' English class perform a scene from *The Bear*.

is up to you. Maybe you want to write quotes, questions, lists, favorite sentences, summaries, arguments for or against things, predictions, new vocabulary words, or maybe you want to draw pictures, write poems or journal entries, or even write about how you identify with a certain character or how an experience that they are going through reminds you of one that you went through. You might want to highlight a certain passage that you really like, or maybe you want to turn the novel into a graphic novel. You might want to tape other texts into your journal. It is up to you."

A look at the syllabus of the global studies class also showed a hefty dose of independent inquiry, especially with the following two objectives:

- Students explain their own perspective on pressing global issues.
- Students present a lesson surrounding a specific global issue and complete a study-designed action plan.

Campfire: Literacy and Food

Joe and Brent have developed an interesting twist on the seminar concept, and they call it "Campfire." Students built the benches that surround the on-campus campfire site, and it is here that they sit around the fire and engage in discussions about a variety of fiction and nonfiction such as Steinbeck's *Grapes of Wrath*, Kaye Gibbons' *Ellen Foster*, Mark Twain's "The Bee"—or online articles about a project by Anna Maria Berry-Jester to find the best burrito in America and the controversy that surrounds her search.

Brent explains that the purpose of Campfire is to "read" food as an extension of the text that they are considering on a given day. "So if we are reading *The Bean Eaters* by Gwendolyn Brooks, we will make a bean salsa with chips and have a chance to talk about beans as a symbol in the poem, beans as characterization and conflict, and talk about all the different ways that beans can be read and can actually take us into the poem." In Campfire activities, text and food are considered as equals.

"We read Maya Angelou's 'I Love the Look of Words' and have popcorn together, and we leave the circle with Angelou's metaphor on our hands and in our brains. The pairing creates more points of entry for the literary works, and it also gets students thinking abstractly in a scaffolded way that allows for some whopper thoughts and connections," said Brent.

Moving discussions into a setting outside of the classroom, especially to one that the students had a hand in developing, provides a venue for these students as authentic as the forum was to Socrates.

A Student Perspective

Part of the *doing* in the social studies class and of the gardening club is to work in the greenhouse and garden that students have built with donations from local businesses. Joe's background in agriculture provides the expertise for these projects, and he has tirelessly written grants to secure funding for the materials.

Quentin Stephenson, a junior who was in the food lit program as a sophomore and is now taking Joe's global studies class, gave me a tour of the greenhouse, raised-bed gardens, and chicken coops (where eggs are sold to the community). He explained that his project for global studies was to research sustainable energy sources and then build a human-powered generator using a bicycle. "And what are you going to do with this project?" I asked, because every project has to demonstrate impact, not just sit as a theoretical study.

"Well, I'd like to build a phone charging station and eventually build a windmill out here as an energy source for the garden. I'm also interested in creating a rain barrel on the back side of the chicken coop." This is a student who said in previous years that he found school boring and wasn't considering college as an option. Now he is taking AP courses in addition to being an active participant in the program, even coming in early to school and spending some weekends working in the garden.

"Everyone wants to see their work go toward something," he said, "and in this class, my work counts."

This statement, perhaps more than any other I heard, exemplifies the philosophy of the program—learning while doing with the added advantage of seeing how learning can make a difference in the community

"Everyone wants to see their work go toward something and in this class, my work counts," said a student in the food lit class.

Students engage in literacy, using wheelbarrows as chairs.

Brent Peters and Joe Franzen

or the world at large. And all of the students I talked with emphasized the power of collaboration. "We become like family," one said, surrounded by other students in the program who were nodding in agreement.

Collaboration and Community

Community is, indeed, the hallmark of this program. Whether students are reading, discussing articles, or actively involved in working, the tenets of community—respect, responsibility, interdependence, and coming to care about each another—are embedded in all learning. Brent says that collaboration is nonnegotiable, and it begins by helping students come to know each other as people.

Class Meals: A Metaphor for Community

The cornerstone of this initiative is the "class community meals" where students bring a variety of dishes and then eat together at one long table. They generally have three large class meals over the course of the year. The first is from the school garden, where students make the meal together as a class. For anything they have not grown, they create a "grocery list" that they take home and fill from their own pantries. "We connect home and school and see the meal as a store of connections that allow us to work together and create a class experience," Joe said.

Meal two is usually a potluck. "We ask students to invite a family member, mentor, or other significant person to join our meal at school. We bring our favorite dishes and share both food and reflection. Turnout is great, and a lot of family members mention that the meal provides them with one of the very few occasions to be at school during the school day. Students create the dining space and table decorations, and we all say a word of thanks and have time to share photos of the class," said Brent.

Meal three is a celebratory picnic and grill-out. This year it will be a barbeque where all the classes come together for the first time to reflect on the year.

Brent and Joe explain that the classroom dynamic can become much like a dinner table where everyone shares, listens, laughs, and where new knowledge becomes a natural part of the conversation. This goes back to the ideas of Michael Pollan, food culture author, who says that the dinner table is a democratic space.

Brent Peters and Joe Franzen

Food Lit students come to know each other by sharing a meal several times a year.

"We try to make our classroom like one big dinner table. And that table can be outside under an oak tree, in the school garden, in the school room, at a class meal, or in an online space," the teachers say. The events promote a sense of caring for one another that enables students to take risks, become vulnerable, accept when they are wrong about something, and, as Brent says, "embrace a willingness to be in a process of growth by shedding the obstacles that come from a fear to explore due to doubt."

Service-Learning at Home

When I visited the campus, the juniors and seniors in Joe's global issues class were using the kitchen to bake a variety of breakfast food for the school's juniors who would be taking the ACT the next day. Students planned to come in early to serve the test takers. While such a project is not long term, students still realized the advantages of service-learning: participating in disciplinary learning to address a genuine need. But Brent pointed out that students were also in service to each other. "We usually think of service-learning as something that we have to leave the school to do. But we can always serve each other if we care about each other. Really care. We can see how making the case for food literacy is also making the case for compassion in the curriculum—and this, we all can agree, is proof that we can not only work toward mastery of the standards but can actually go way beyond any set of standards to the fabric of what enables students to care about learning for learning's sake and about learning to allow actions that will build confidence, connection, investment, and empowerment."

Cross-Culture Connections

One of the most unique aspects of this initiative, a cross-culture exchange relationship between the students at Fern Creek and the Navajo Nation, has become a national model of collaboration. Brent, who is a graduate student at Middlebury Bread Loaf School of English, met vice president of the Navajo Nation, Rex Lee Jim, when he was visiting Bread Loaf three years ago. Brent began telling him about the program at Fern Creek High and, with "the immense support the Middlebury Bread Loaf community," says Brent, "the collaboration began."

Brent Peters and Joe Franzen

Students in Joe Franzen's class bake breakfast bread for classmates who are taking the ACT.

Perhaps the story is best told on the website created by Brent, Joe, Paul Barnwell, English and digital literacy teacher, and the students. The site continues to be maintained by students from the Navajo Nation and Fern Creek High School students.

From Navajo Kentuckians at navajokentuckians.com:

> On February 26, 2013, several students and staff from Fern Creek High School embarked on a life changing journey. Earlier, in late 2012, Brent Peters, an English and Food Lit teacher, sat in a room with Rex Lee Jim, the vice president of the Navajo Nation, and discussed the philosophy behind the class Food Lit. Vice President Jim was intrigued and invited Brent, his fellow teacher Joe Franzen, and a group of students to visit the Navajo Nation to hold a conference on Food Lit called "In the Garden of the Home God." Through the conference, students and teachers from both parties have built strong bonds.

Brent describes the experience as a powerful example of combining literacies. "Students were able to 'read' their communities, their families, their stories, as well as farms, chefs, farmers, elders, foods of all types—and take these readings to be able to produce many different texts, which included poetry, digital stories, public speaking, essays, letters, a digital space, photographs, meals, and more. "

Hear students describe the experience in their own words through a video at navajokentuckians.com/thank-you/ where they talk about how their perspectives have changed in ways they never could have predicted and how food-related issues connect them both to "home" and to each other.

Students from the Navajo nation, a semiautonomous nation within the United States located in northeastern Arizona, northwestern New Mexico, and southeastern Utah, have since reciprocated by visiting Fern Creek to continue the ongoing project of conducting action research in communities. Their ambitious goals include making a difference in their own backyards by studying the effect of food on poverty, health, home, education, and access. The students from two completely different regions of the country spent time with each other for social, altruistic, and academic reasons, and the resulting experience taught them much more than they could have learned in any single classroom.

Since its inception, Joe and Brent's students (known as Navajo Kentuckians) join Navajo students, teachers, and Rex Lee Jim to present

We can not only work toward mastery of the standards but can actually go way beyond any set of standards to the fabric of what enables students to care about learning for learning's sake.

at various locations such as Middlebury College, National Council of Teachers of English, National Indian Health Board, and the Smithsonian. The two groups continue to collaborate, often via Skype, "to ensure that students share stories and speak to the ways that their research in their communities changed them and brought them together as a family."

Brent says that the best part of the project has been not only the ways that students come to validate the voice inside of them, but in the ways that the experiences have allowed students to also welcome other communities in. "Food Lit matters because people and their relationship with food matters—everywhere, " he explains.

These students, many of whom had never before been out of their own states, experienced cross-culture literacy because they lived it as opposed to reading about it.

They acted as scientists, sociologists, anthropologists, historians, writers, and readers engaged in real-world work. Their experiences exemplify disciplinary literacy because they used the tools that experts in the field use. While they may not be able to count the standards they covered, their teachers and administrators could, no doubt, tick them off.

Brent Peters and Joe Franzen

Fliers such as this hang on the walls of Brent and Joe's classrooms, reminding students of the rich experiences they have had in the food lit program.

An Administrative Perspective

Assistant principal Rebecca Nichols, a pragmatist, notes that the beauty of the initiative lay with these two teachers taking "the idea of community and exploding it," but make no mistake, if the test scores had not supported their efforts, there would be no program. "We rely on numbers and covering curriculum" and that must come first, like it or not. The first year began with a single course, and then, as students' test scores, attendance, and engagement increased, it slowly expanded from one course to eight in-school courses and countless hours of student learning outside of school. Rebecca admitted that initially she was surprised at the unprecedented success of the initiative but now expects that the program will continue to grow.

Students as Learners, Students as Presenters

How did I come to know about this unique and successful experiment? I had keynoted the 2015 Kentucky Council of Teachers of English's Conference, and as I was waiting to do a breakout session, I heard that students were holding small-group discussions with teachers. I peeked into a room with a sign on the door designating the session as "Food Lit" and, inside, I saw five sets of students speaking with animation to teachers seated around tables. The teachers were listening intently and asking questions before rotating on to the next group.

What I heard from students was astonishing. "I never thought of myself as a writer; actually, I wasn't a very good writer—and now I'm in AP English because I found my voice when reading and writing about food," said one young woman who appeared completely comfortable talking in front of adults. A student I discussed earlier in this chapter, Quentin, talked about how his entire view of food had changed once he started growing it himself because, as he pointed out, "Growing a tomato isn't easy." He picked up an egg from the table and began talking about what he had learned when he did research in order to care for the chickens students were raising. "One thing that stayed with me," he said, "is that thousands of them are often crammed into trucks destined to be fast food."

Another pair of students discussed argumentative essays and how it was easier to write when you really knew about the subject through hours of reading, researching and *doing*. They described an experience in Brent's English class where they wrote about whether or not a fictitious manufacturing complex, DFE Bottlers, a corn syrup refinery and bottling plant, should be allowed to construct its facility in a made-up city called Panzenland.

These students, many of whom had never before been out of their own states, experienced cross-culture literacy because they lived it as opposed to reading about it.

Teacher Brent Peters, second row, far left, and Joe Franzen, kneeling on right, pose with students at the conference hotel where they had presented a session about food lit and Navajo Kentuckians.

We debated the issue in Panzenland at a Town Meeting format. From here, we either voted for or against DFE Bottlers, and the motion passed. Some classes decided on the bottlers, and some did not, and it was interesting to see how the personalities of the groups helped to influence the final vote. Also, Mr. Franzen and Mr. Peters were both given roles as characters in the town who represented opposing sides. We had former members of the Food Lit class, now juniors, who got permission from their teachers to come back to our Panzenland scenario in their previous personas to help explain how it worked. They sort of "handed down" the activity to us.

A teacher at the table asked what they had read and discussed in preparation for this activity and together they ticked off texts:

- *Hansel and Gretel* by the Brothers Grimm
- Chapters from *The Road* by Cormac McCarthy
- A short story by Sandra Cisneros

- An essay titled "Yes, Sugar Is Poison But That's OK" by Jodi Bartle
- An essay titled "These People Need a Lot of Things but They Don't Need a Coke" by Michael Moss

I was struck with how the first speaker turned often to her partner, a young man, and asked for his input or confirmation. They spoke together easily, sharing the stage and honoring each other's contributions.

When I later asked Brent why the "Panzenland" activity was so valuable, he explained, "We engaged the students in a discussion about what they learned and looked at our experience on the metacognitive level to see how we were synthesizing ideas. Students experienced an authentic situation where they had to vote and stand up for a side that they would have normally disagreed with or that went against their own personal beliefs. But, given the circumstances and the personas they created, each voted true to their persona. The big idea here was understanding opposing perspectives and creating counterclaims in argument to engage different viewpoints."

Students were acting as apprentices in a real-world setting, constructing and applying knowledge, learning from each other, and asking for help when needed.

The Power of Disciplinary Literacy

I was so impressed with what I had just heard from the food lit students that I had trouble getting into the topic of "textbook fatigue" at my next session and spent half of my allotted time talking about how the program demonstrated the type of deep and sustainable learning I envisioned when I thought about what was possible in education. I then changed my travel plans so that I could visit the school before returning home to Atlanta.

While at Fern Creek High School, I sat in on classes and talked to students, most of whom could barely contain their enthusiasm for the evidence of learning that surrounded us. The walls were covered with student work (ongoing as well as completed), students discussed (and showed me) their many projects, and teachers demonstrated how literacy had become an intrinsic tool for work in their disciplines. In fact, students were acting as apprentices in a real-world setting, constructing and applying knowledge, learning from each other, and asking for help when needed from their "expert" teachers—while respecting the contributions of everyone.

Brent Peters and Joe Franzen

I listen and take notes as students at Fern Creek High School share their experiences in the food lit program.

I share this program in Kentucky not as a model for replication but as an example of what is possible when teachers come together, working only with what they have, to create a meaningful educational experience that challenges, engages, teaches, and literally transforms students. Maybe food lit isn't appropriate for your population (though it certainly is a universal theme in literature and in life), but the principles demonstrated in this school of "learning through doing" can be adapted by any teacher, team, department, school, or district. All it takes is a readjustment of our view of teaching, learning, and literacy.

WORKING FOR KNOWLEDGE

In the foreword to *Content Matters* (McConachie & Petrosky, 2010), Lauren Resnick makes two points that could serve as mission statements for the program at Fern Creek High as well as for the theme of this book. She writes, "The only knowledge that will stick, that will be available to build on next month or next year (or in college), is knowledge that a student has worked to understand." And she reminds us that students are motivated for further academic work when "they are treated as intelligent people who come to class with knowledge and reasoning skills. Everyone benefits from this reintellectualization of school work that moves it away from the generic and remedial and brings it back to the disciplines" (viii).

Indeed, disciplinary literacy is the only paradigm that really makes sense for today's teachers and students: reading, writing, thinking, and doing . . . content area by content area.

REFERENCES

Almossawi, A. (2014). *An illustrated book of bad arguments*. New York, NY: The Experiment.

Anderson, R. C., Wilson, P. T., & Fielding, L. G. (1988). Growth in reading and how children spend their time outside of school. *Reading Research Quarterly, 23*(3), 285–303.

Applebee, A. N., & Langer, J. A. (2013). *Writing instruction that works: Proven methods for middle and high school classrooms*. New York, NY: Teachers College Press.

Armstrong, J. (2005). *Photo by Brady: A picture of the Civil War*. New York, NY: Atheneum Books for Young Readers.

Banchi, H., & Bell, R. (2008). The many levels of inquiry. *Science and Children, 46*(2), 26–29.

Bellanca, J. A. (Ed.). (2015). *Deeper learning: Beyond 21st century skills*. Bloomington, IN: Solution Tree Press.

Bender, W. H. (2012). *Project-based learning: Differentiating instruction for the 21st century*. Thousand Oaks, CA: Corwin.

Bragg, G. (2011). *How they croaked: The awful ends of the awfully famous*. New York, NY: Walker Publishing.

Burke, J. (2010). *What's the big idea? Question-driven units to motivate reading, writing, and thinking*. Portsmouth, NH: Heinemann.

Burns, M. (2014, October). Uncovering the math curriculum. *Educational Leadership, 72*(2), 64–68.

Cell Press. (2014, October 2). How curiosity changes the brain to enhance learning. *ScienceDaily*. Retrieved from www.sciencedaily.com/releases/2014/10/141002123631.htm

Costa, A. L., & Kallick, B. (2009). *Learning and leading with habits of mind*. Alexandria, VA: ASCD.

Cunningham, A. E., & Stanovich, K. E. (1991). Tracking the unique effects of print exposure in children: Associations with vocabulary, general knowledge, and spelling. *Journal of Educational Psychology, 83*(2), 264–274.

Daniels, H., & Daniels, E. (2013). *The best-kept teaching secret: How written conversations engage kids, activate learning, grow fluent writers . . . K–12*. Thousand Oaks, CA: Corwin.

Daniels, H., & Steineke, N. (2014). *Teaching the social skills of academic interaction, grades 4–12: Step-by-step lessons for respect, responsibility, and results*. Thousand Oaks, CA: Corwin.

Darling-Hammond, L., Barron, B., Pearson, P. D., Schoenfeld, A. H., Stage, E. K., Zimmerman, T. D., . . . & Tilson, J. L. (2008). *Powerful learning: What we know about teaching for understanding*. San Francisco, CA: Jossey-Bass.

Diamond, J. E., & Gaier Knapik, M. C. (2014). *Literacy lessons for a digital world: Using blogs, wikis, podcasts, and more to meet the demands of the Common Core*. New York, NY: Scholastic.

Donovan, M. S., & Bransford, J. D. (Eds.). (2005). *How students learn: Science in the classroom*. Washington, DC: National Academies Press, National Research Council.

Draper, R. J. (2015, March). Using the Common Core State Standards to support disciplinary literacies. *Voices from the Middle, 22*(3), 59.

Ellison, K., & Freedberg, L. (2015, April 27). *Project-based learning on the rise under Common Core*. EdSource. Retrieved from http://edsource.org/2015/project-based-learning-on-the-rise-under-the-common-core/78851#.VUOMDdFFAdU

Ferling, J. (2010, January). *Myths of the American Revolution*. Smithsonian.com. Retrieved from http://www.smithsonianmag.com/history/myths-of-the-american-revolution-10941835/?+Archaeology+%7C+Smithsonian.com%29=&utm_campaign=Feed%3A+smithsonianmag%2Fhistory-archaeology+%28History+&page=1&no-ist=

Fisher, D., & Frey, N. (2014). *Text-dependent questions: Pathways to close and critical reading, grades 6–12*. Thousand Oaks, CA: Corwin.

Fox, D. (2015, January 21). *Fish live beneath Antarctica*. Retrieved from http://www.nature.com/news/fish-live-beneath-antarctica-1.16772

Greaney, V. (1980). Factors related to amount and type of leisure time reading. *Reading Research Quarterly, 15*(3), 337–357.

Guthrie, J. T. (2007). *Engaging adolescents in reading*. Thousand Oaks, CA: Corwin.

Guys Read: http://guysread.com

Helterbran, V. R. (2012). *Why rattlesnakes rattle . . . and 250 other things you should know*. Lanham, MD: Taylor Trade.

Humphreys, C., & Parker, R. (2015). *Making number talks matter: Developing mathematical practices and deepening understanding*. Portland, ME: Stenhouse.

Janeczko, P. B. (2012). *The dark game: True spy stories from invisible ink to CIA moles.* Somerville, MA: Candlewick Press.

Jetton, T. L., & Shanahan, C. (2012). *Adolescent literacy in the academic disciplines: General principles and practical strategies.* New York, NY: Guilford Press.

Krashen, S. D. (2004). *The power of reading: Insights from the research* (2nd ed.). Westport, CT: Libraries Unlimited.

Langer, J. A. (2011). *Envisioning knowledge: Building literacy in the academic disciplines.* New York, NY: Teachers College Press.

Lent, R. C. (2010, September). The responsibility breakthrough. *Educational Leadership, 68*(1), 68–71.

Lent, R. C. (2012). *Overcoming textbook fatigue: 21st century tools to revitalize teaching and learning.* Alexandria, VA: ASCD.

Lent, R. C., & Gilmore, B. (2013). *Common Core CPR: What about the adolescents who struggle . . . or just don't care?* Thousand Oaks, CA: Corwin.

Lesh, B. (2011). *Why won't you just tell us the answer? Teaching historical thinking in grades 7–12.* Portland, ME: Stenhouse.

Levitt, S. D., & Dubner, S. J. (2010). *Freakonomics* (Vol. 61). Milan, Italy: Sperling & Kupfer.

Lewis, W. E., Walpole, S., & McKenna, M. C. (2013). *Cracking the Common Core: Choosing and using texts in grades 6–12.* New York, NY: Guilford Press.

Linn, M. C., Davis, E. A., & Eylon, B. (2004). The scaffolded knowledge integration framework for instruction. In M. C. Linn, E. A. Davis, & P. Bell (Eds.), *Internet environments for science education* (pp. 47–72). Mahwah, NJ: Lawrence Erlbaum.

Lockhart, E. (2014). *We were liars.* New York, NY: Delacorte Press.

Loewen, J. W. (2007). *Lies my teacher told me: Everything your American history book got wrong.* New York, NY: Touchstone.

Lorenzi, R. (2014, October 20). *King Tut re-creation presents a shocking image.* Discovery News Retrieved from http://news.discovery.com/history/archaeology/king-tut-re-creation-presents-a-shocking-image-141020.htm

Lou, Y., Abrami, P., Spence, J., Poulsen, C., Chambers, B., & d'Apollonia, S. (1996). Within-class grouping: A meta-analysis. *Review of Educational Research, 71,* 449–521.

Manderino, M., & Wickens, C. (2014). Addressing disciplinary literacy in the Common Core Standards. *Illinois Council of Reading Journal, 42*(2), 28–39.

Marshall, J. C. (2013). *Succeeding with inquiry in science and math classrooms.* Alexandria, VA: ASCD.

Martinez, M. R., & McGrath, D. (2014). *Deeper learning: How eight innovative public schools are transforming education in the twenty-first century.* New York, NY: The New Press.

Marzano, R. J., Pickering, D., & Pollock, J. E. (2001). *Classroom instruction that works: Research-based strategies for increasing student achievement.* Arlington, VA: ASCD.

Mastroianni, M. P. (2013). Writing in mathematics. In A. N. Applebee & J. A. Langer (Eds.), *Writing instruction that works: Proven methods for middle and high school classrooms* (pp. 71–93). New York, NY: Teachers College Press.

McConachie, S. M., & Petrosky, A. R. (Eds.). (2010). *Content matters: A disciplinary literacy approach to improving student learning.* San Francisco, CA: Jossey-Bass.

McMillan, J. H. (2007). Formative classroom assessment: The key to improving student achievement. In J. H. McMillan (Ed.), *Formative classroom assessment: Theory into practice* (pp. 1–7). New York, NY: Teachers College Press.

McTighe, J., & Wiggins, G. (2013). *Essential questions: Opening doors to student understanding.* Alexandria, VA: ASCD.

Michaels, S., O'Connor, M. C., Hall, M. W., & Resnick. L. B. (2002). *Accountable talk: Classroom conversation that works.* Pittsburgh, PA: University of Pittsburgh. Retrieved from http://ifl.pitt.edu/index.php/educator_resources/accountable_talk

Moje, E. B. (2010, April 6). *Disciplinary literacy: Why it matters and what you should do about it.* Retrieved from https://www.youtube.com/watch?v=Id4gKJ-wGzU

Munroe, R. (2014). *What if?: Serious scientific answers to absurd hypothetical questions.* New York, NY: Houghton Mifflin.

Nachowitz, M. (2013). Writing in science. In A. N. Applebee & J. A. Langer, *Writing instruction that works: Proven methods for middle and high school classrooms* (pp. 94–110). New York, NY: Teachers College Press.

National Academy of Sciences. (2012). *A framework for K–12 science education.* Retrieved from http://www.nextgenscience.org/next-generation-science-standards

National Commission on Writing in America's Schools and Colleges. (2003). *The neglected "R": The need for a writing revolution.* Retrieved from www.collegeboard.com/prod_downloads/writingcom/neglectedr.pdf

National Council of Teachers of English. (2008). *Writing now: An NCTE research policy brief.* Urbana, IL: Author.

National Council of Teachers of English. (2011). *Literacies of discipline* [Policy brief]. Urbana, IL: NCTE, James R. Squire Office of Policy Research.

National Council of Teachers of Social Studies. (2008). *A vision of powerful teaching and learning in the social studies: Building social understanding and civic efficacy.* Washington, DC: Author.

Newkirk, T. (2014). *Minds made for stories: How we really read and write informational and persuasive texts.* Portsmouth, NH: Heinemann.

Newmann, F. M., & Wehlage, G. G. (1993, April). Five standards of authentic instruction. *Educational Leadership, 50*(7), 8–12.

O'Brien, T. (2009). *The things they carried.* New York, NY: Houghton Mifflin.

Olson, S., & Loucks-Horsley, S. (Eds.). (2000). *Inquiry and the National Science Education Standards: A guide for teaching and learning.* Washington, DC: National Academies Press.

Palincsar, A. S. (1986). Reciprocal teaching. In *Teaching reading as thinking.* Oak Brook, IL: North Central Regional Educational Laboratory.

Park, A. (2015, February 23). New ways to disrupt aging. *Time, 185*(6), 72–76.

Pink, D. H. (2011). *Drive: The surprising truth about what motivates us.* New York, NY: Riverhead Books.

Posamentier, A. S., & Lehmann, I. (2014). *Mathematical curiosities: A treasure trove of unexpected entertainments.* Amherst, NY: Prometheus Books.

Ravi, A. K. (2010). Disciplinary literacy in the history classroom. In S. M. McConachie & A. R. Petrosky (Eds.), *Content matters: A disciplinary literacy approach to improving students learning* (pp. 33–61). San Francisco, CA: Jossey-Bass.

Roberts, T., & Billings, L. (2011). *Teaching critical thinking: Using seminars for 21st century literacy.* Larchmont, NY: Eye on Education.

Rose, C. M., & Arline, C. B. (Eds.). (2009). *Uncovering student thinking in mathematics: Grades 6–12.* Thousand Oaks, CA: Corwin.

Roth, K., Marshall, J. C., Taylor, J. A., Wilson, C., & Hvidsten, C. (2014, April). *Impact of science professional development on student learning: Four studies awaken dialogue.* Paper presented at the National Association for Research in Science Teaching, Pittsburgh, PA.

Rothstein, A. S., Rothstein, E. B., & Lauber, G, (2006). *Write for mathematics.* Thousand Oaks, CA: Corwin.

Shanahan, T., & Shanahan, C. (2012).What is disciplinary literacy and why does it matter? *Topics in Language Disorders, 32*(1), 7–18.

Stanovich, K. E., & Cunningham, A. E. (1993). Where does knowledge come from? Specific associations between print exposure and information acquisition. *Journal of Educational Psychology, 85*(2), 211.

Tammet, D. (2012). *Thinking in numbers: How math illuminates our lives.* London, UK: Hodder & Stoughton.

Werlin, N. (2005). *Double helix.* New York, NY: Puffin Books.

Wilberding, E. (2014). *Teach like Socrates: Guiding Socratic dialogues & discussions in the classroom.* Waco, TX: Prufrock Press.

Wilhelm, J. (2008). *Engaging readers and writers with inquiry: Promoting deep understandings in the language arts and the content areas.* New York, NY: Scholastic.

Wilhelm, J. D., & Smith, M. W. (with Fransen, S.). (2014). *Reading unbound: Why kids need to read what they want—and why we should let them.* New York, NY: Scholastic.

Willis, J. (2011, July 11). *The brain-based benefits of writing for math and science learning.* Retrieved from http://www.edutopia.org/blog/writing-executive-function-brain-research-judy-willis

Wineburg, S., Martin, D., & Monte-Sano, C. (2013). *Reading like a historian: Teaching literacy in middle and high school history classroom*s. New York, NY: Teachers College Press.

INDEX

Figures are indicated by f following the page number.

TED Talk, 113
10 Questions, 42
Textbooks, inadequacies of, 24
Text selection, 25–26, 25f, 29, 32
The Dark Game: True Spy Stories from Invisible Ink to CIA Moles (Janeczko), 131
Thinking as a skeptic, 124–126, 125f
Think-pair-share, 153
Tiger Rising (DiCamillo), 41
Timed essays, 72
Time magazine, 42, 54
Time spent reading, 22, 23f, 57f
Topic selection, 136
To Read or Not to Read study, 22
Tsarnaev, Dzhokhar, 89
Turn and talk strategy, 31
Tut, King, 34–36
Tutorials, 157
Twitter, reading within disciplines and, 37–38, 38f
Two-column writing, 70–71

Ullrich Sherman, Carlynn, 27
"Uncovering the Math Curriculum" (Burns), 110
University of California curiosity study, 128–129
University of Pittsburgh's Learning Research and Development Center, 5

Victoria, letter to Mary Todd Lincoln, 86, 86f
Video tutorials, 157
Visual literacy, 42–47, 45–46f
Vlogs, 140
Vocabulary, 149–152
Vocabulary IS Comprehension: Getting to the Root of Text Complexity (Robb), 150

Walker, Alice, 90
Washington, George, 56
Wehlage, Gary, 180–181
Weisenburger, Kurt, 37–38
Weiss, Stephanie, 21, 161
We Were Liars (Lockhart), 132

"Whaling is a Big Issue" infographic, 46–47, 46f
"What Is the Value of Life? And Other Socratic Questions" (Cuny), 178–179
"When is Cheryl's birthday?" 34
"Why is Measles So Contagious?," 127
Why War is Never a Good Idea (Walker), 90
Wide reading, 22–24
Wilhelm, Jeffrey, 36–37
Williams Hall, Megan, 162–163
Willis, Judy, 63
Word exposure, 22, 23f
World Forum, 180
Write outs, 189
Writer's block, bell-ringer questions and answers and, 83–85, 84f
Writing Instruction That Works (Applebee & Langer), 90
Writing within disciplines
    assessment and, 74–75, 76f, 80, 98
    bell-ringer questions and answers, 83–85, 84f
    benefits of, 63
    blogs and, 95–100, 97–98f
    from content to story, 92–95, 93f
    differentiated learning logs, 80–83, 82f
    English language arts, 71–73
    grammar and spelling issues, 80
    history, 66–67
    math, 68–71, 69f, 71f, 79, 79f
    need for, 61–62
    purposes of, 78
    quickjots, 91–92, 92f
    read/think/respond, 85–87, 86f, 88f
    rubrics, 75–77
    science, 65–66, 77, 95, 95f
    shifts for implementing, 63–65
    social studies, 66–67
    standards and, 63–64
    talk back, 87–91

Yeager, Nicolas, 24f, 56f

Zenner, Colleen, 62f, 77, 108f, 145–147
Zink, Albert, 36

CORWIN LITERACY

ReLeah Lent's Workshop on Disciplinary Literacy: Deeper Learning *Within* the Disciplines

ReLeah Lent provides keynotes, workshops, and residencies for content-area teachers and entire faculties designed to help them identify and develop discipline-specific literacy tools. By working with colleagues both within and across disciplines, teachers learn how to utilize literacy to deepen students' understandings in their own specific subjects.

- **Science:** How do students read with a questioning stance and write to explain?
- **History:** How do students approach primary sources and develop arguments?
- **Math:** How do students adopt the literacy habits of mathematicians?
- **English:** How do students read closely and write with elaboration?

"I continue to be amazed at the passion, joy, reflection, and confidence ReLeah inspires in teachers of all disciplines. We have teachers on a waiting list and teachers asking to continue to learn with her year after year. I've never experienced a professional development initiative that has sparked such enthusiasm and commitment!"

—**Marsha Voigt,** Literacy Coach

To book your consulting days with ReLeah Lent, call **800-831-6640**

BECAUSE ALL
TEACHERS
ARE LEADERS

A SAGE Company

Helping educators make the greatest impact

CORWIN HAS ONE MISSION: to enhance education through intentional professional learning.

We build long-term relationships with our authors, educators, clients, and associations who partner with us to develop and continuously improve the best evidence-based practices that establish and support lifelong learning.